Well Read 4

SKILLS AND STRATEGIES FOR READING

Mindy Pasternak | Elisaveta Wrangell

OXFORD
UNIVERSITY PRESS

OXFORD
UNIVERSITY PRESS

198 Madison Avenue
New York, NY 10016 USA

Great Clarendon Street, Oxford OX2 6DP UK

Oxford University Press is a department of the University of Oxford.
It furthers the University's objective of excellence in research, scholarship,
and education by publishing worldwide in

Oxford New York

Auckland Cape Town Dar es Salaam Hong Kong Karachi
Kuala Lumpur Madrid Melbourne Mexico City Nairobi
New Delhi Shanghai Taipei Toronto

With offices in

Argentina Austria Brazil Chile Czech Republic France Greece
Guatemala Hungary Italy Japan Poland Portugal Singapore
South Korea Switzerland Thailand Turkey Ukraine Vietnam

OXFORD and OXFORD ENGLISH are registered trademarks of
Oxford University Press

© Oxford University Press 2007

Database right Oxford University Press (maker)

Executive Publisher: Janet Aitchison
Senior Acquisitions Editor: Pietro Alongi
Editor: Phebe W. Szatmari
Editorial Assistant: Beverley Langevine
Art Director: Maj Hagsted
Senior Designer: Claudia Carlson
Production Layout Artist: Colleen Ho
Art Editor: Robin Fadool
Production Manager: Shanta Persaud
Production Controller: Eve Wong

ISBN: 978 0 19 476106 2

Printed in Hong Kong

10 9 8 7 6 5 4 3 2 1

ACKNOWLEDGMENTS

Cover art: Claudia Carlson

The publisher would like to thank the following for their permission
to reproduce copyright material: **pp. 4-5**, "Hollywood-motion pictures"
by Tino Balio. Copyright © 1995 by *The UNESCO Courier*. Reprinted and
adapted with permission. **pp. 8-9**, "Director envisions her film as proto-
type for Jordanian Cinema" by Natasha Twal Tynes. Copyright © 2003 by
Natasha Twal Tynes. Reprinted and adapted with permission. **pp. 14-16**,
"Bollywood Bonanza" by Nick Goodway. Copyright © 2004 by *The Evening
Standard*. Reprinted and adapted with permission. **pp. 23-24**, "Online
Dating Do's and Don'ts" by Pepper Schwartz, PhD. Copyright © 2004
by Lifetimetv.com. Reprinted and adapted with permission. **pp. 29-30**,
"Smelling out your perfect mate" by Paul Carey. Copyright © 2004 by
Western Mail UK. Reprinted and adapted with permission. **pp. 36-38**,
"Meeting Strangers: Proximity and Emotions" from Baron, R. A. & Byrne,
D. *Social Psychology, 8/e* (c) 1997. Published by Allyn and Bacon, Boston, MA.
Copyright © by Pearson Education. Reprinted and adapted by permission

of the publisher. **pp. 45-46**, "One man's junk is another man's treasure:
China talking trash" by InTech Magazine Staff. Copyright © 2003 by *InTech
News*. Reprinted and adapted with permission. **pp. 51-53**, "These 'shop-
pers' refuse to curb their enthusiasm" by Jan Uebelherr. Copyright ©
2004 by *Milwaukee Journal Sentinel*. Reprinted and adapted with permission.
pp. 60-61, "Building Tires: One UA Researcher Has High Hopes for Scrap
Tires" by David Barber. Copyright © 2002 by *Report on Research*, University
of Arizona. Reprinted and adapted with permission. **pp. 69-70**, "Alumnus
admits smuggling Iraqi artifacts" by Hannah Charlick. Copyright © 2004
by The Daily Princetonian Publishing Company, Inc. Reprinted and adapted
with permission. **pp. 74-75**, "Alexander's army marches again" by Hugh
Hart. Copyright © 2004 by Hugh Hart. Reprinted and adapted with permission. **pp. 83-85**, "First City in the New World" by John F. Ross. Copyright
© 2002 by John F. Ross. Originally appeared in *Smithsonian*, August 2002.
Reprinted and adapted with permission. **pp. 93-94**, "Psychic for Cops"
by Bill Lagattuta. Copyright © 2000 by CBS News. Reprinted and adapted
with permission. **pp. 98-99**, "A Sixth Sense" by Vicki Mabrey. Copyright ©
2002 by CBS News. Reprinted and adapted with permission. **pp. 106-108**,
"Pattern and Circumstance: The Power of Coincidence" by Jill Neimark.
Copyright © 2004 by *Psychology Today*. Reprinted and adapted with permis-
sion. **pp. 117-118**, "Young dreams: local professionals give guidance to
adolescent entrepreneurs" by Rebecca Markway. Copyright © 2003 by
Greater Baton Rouge Business Report. Reprinted and adapted with permission.
pp. 124-125, "Is Corporate Social Responsibility an Oxymoron?" by Lois
A. Levin/Robert C. Hinkley. Copyright © 2004 by CommonDreams.org.
Reprinted and adapted with permission. **pp. 133-135**, "Putting on a New
Face: The Creation of a Caring Corporation" excerpt from *Unstoppable: 45
Powerful Stories of Perseverance and Triumph from People Just Like You* by Cynthia
Kersey. Copyright © 1998 by Sourcebooks, Inc. Reprinted and adapted with
permission **pp. 143-144**, "Mediterranean Diet Linked to Longer Life" by
Salynn Boyles. Copyright © 2005 by WebMd, Inc. Reprinted with permis-
sion. **pp. 150-151**, "Soy: It does a body good" by Psychology Today Staff.
Copyright © 2004 by *Psychology Today*. Reprinted and adapted with permis-
sion. **pp. 158-161**, "Thai Fire" excerpted from *Thailand Confidential* by Jerry
Hopkins. Copyright © 2005 by Tuttle Publishing. Reprinted and adapted
with permission. **pp. 167-168**, "Animal Testing Continues at U. (Only used
when other options exhausted)" by Jessica Ansert. Copyright © 2005 by
The Daily Targum. Reprinted and adapted with permission. **pp. 172-174**,
"Animal-Human Hybrids Spark Controversy" by Maryann Mott. Copyright ©
2005 by National Geographic. Reprinted and adapted with permission. **pp.
180-182**, "Creating the Stuff of Life" by Steve Connor. Copyright © 2005 by
The Independent. Reprinted and adapted with permission.

The authors and publisher would like to acknowledge the following indi-
viduals for their invaluable input during the development of this series:
Macarena Aguilar, Cy-Fair College, TX; Sharon Allerson, East Los Angeles
College, CA; Susan Niemeyer, Los Angeles City College, CA; Elaine S. Paris,
Koc University, Istanbul, Turkey; Sylvia Cavazos Pena, University of Texas
at Brownsville, TX; Maggy Sami Saba, King Abdulaziz University, Jeddah,
Kingdom of Saudi Arabia; Stephanie Toland, North Side Learning Center,
MN; Jay Myoung Yu, Yonsei University at Wonju, Korea; Anthony Zak,
Universitas Sam Ratulangi, Manado, Indonesia.

Special thanks go to Barbara Rifkind for her support of the editorial team.

AUTHOR ACKNOWLEDGMENTS

We express our sincere thanks to Peggy Cleve, without whose prompting
and guidance, this series would not have been written. We also thank our
families and the following friends and colleagues for their encouragement,
advice, and support: H. Douglas Brown, Wendy Crockett, Sheila Dwight,
François Hervé, Lee Egerman, Paolo Longoni, Dave Myers, Don Orf, Patricia
Porter, and Deborah vanDommelen. We are furthermore grateful to the
students at the University of California, Riverside's International Education
Programs for their invaluable input in the development of this series. Finally,
we thank Phebe Szatmari and Pietro Alongi, and the Oxford University Press
editorial and design staff for their hard work on this series.

Notes to the Teacher

Welcome to *Well Read*, a four-level series that teaches and reinforces crucial reading skills and vocabulary strategies step-by-step through a wide range of authentic texts that are meant to engage students' (and teachers') interest. *Well Read 4* is intended for students at the high-intermediate to low-advanced level.

Each of the eight chapters in the book revolves around a central theme, but every text in a chapter approaches the theme from a different angle or level of formality. This provides multiple insights into the subject matter, while at the same time developing reading skills. Thus, students will be able to approach the theme with increasing fluency.

Well Read is designed so that all the activities, including reading, are broken up into smaller pieces, and each has specific goals so that all students, regardless of their individual level, can participate and succeed. The activities in the book support the approach that students do *not* have to understand every word of a text in order to understand its basic themes. Vocabulary strategies in each chapter allow students to feel more comfortable guessing the meanings of unfamiliar words or phrases based on their context.

Chapter Introduction

The opening page introduces the chapter's theme. Questions and photographs are designed to activate the students' prior knowledge, as well as stimulate some limited discussion before the previewing, reading, and post-reading activities.

Getting Started

This activity precedes each text or graphic component. It is designed to help students focus in on a more specific topic through reflection and discussion. It also introduces a small number of critical vocabulary words or phrases.

Active Previewing

Active Previewing asks students to read only brief and selected parts of the text, and then answer very simple questions that focus on this material. This activity encourages the notion that students do not have to understand each and every word of what they are reading. There is a strong emphasis on how to preview a wide range of genres, both academic and non-academic, including—but not limited to—newspaper articles, online texts, magazine articles, textbook articles, tables, charts, graphs, timelines, and graphics.

Reading and Recalling

The first reading activity asks students to read and recall. This approach is less daunting than being presented with an entire text, and it also allows the students to retain more. Recalling encourages students to be accountable for the material they read. While students build their short-term memories, they begin to process information more quickly and holistically. Perfect recall is never the goal.

Understanding the Text

After each text, students are presented with a two-part reading comprehension activity. The first part checks the students' comprehension of the most basic ideas expressed in the text, whereas the second part challenges the students to recall other key ideas and information.

Reading Skills

Among other essential skills, students are introduced to *Topic, Main Idea,* and *Supporting Details* in separate chapters, which allows them to practice and master each of these skills before progressing to the next. Earlier chapters present choices in a multiple choice fashion, whereas subsequent chapters require the students to write their own interpretations. The ability to think critically about the information that is presented in the text is a crucial part of being an active reader. Students are first taught to distinguish between facts and opinions, and later, inferences. In the final chapters of the textbook, students will be asked to find facts and opinions and to make inferences of their own.

Vocabulary Strategies

Students first learn that they can understand the general idea of a text without understanding every word; however, skipping words is not always an option, thus students are introduced to different strategies throughout the book that can help them determine the meanings of new vocabulary without using their dictionaries. All vocabulary activities use examples from the texts themselves, yet the vocabulary strategies taught can be applied universally to reading that students do outside class. Developing these strategies will allow students to become more autonomous readers.

Discussing the Issues

Every text ends with a series of questions that encourage students to express their opinions and ideas about the general subject discussed in the text. The questions are designed to be communicative in that they strike upon compelling issues raised in the text.

Putting It On Paper

Reading and writing are two skills that inherently go together. The writing activity complements the chapter texts, yet it is also designed to stand independently should the teacher decide not to read all of the chapter texts. Each *Putting It On Paper* activity offers two writing prompts; the teacher can allow students to choose between the prompts or can select one prompt for all students to use.

Taking It Online

Each *Taking It Online* activity guides the students through the steps necessary for conducting online research, based on the theme of the chapter. Teachers might opt to prescreen a select number of websites in advance, thus directing the students to more reliable and useful sites. *Taking It Online* finishes with a follow-up activity that enables the students to take their research one step further, in pairs or groups.

An Answer Key, a PowerPoint® Teaching Tool, and an ExamView Pro® Test Generator with customizable tests and quizzes are also available with each level of *Well Read* in the *Well Read Instructor's Pack*.

Contents

Welcome to *Well Read*

Well Read is a four-level series that develops students' reading skills and vocabulary strategies, preparing them for success in the classroom as critical thinkers.

There are eight chapters in *Well Read* and seven sections in each chapter: *Chapter Introduction, Text 1, Text 2, Text 3, Text 4, Putting It On Paper,* and *Taking It Online.*

Chapter 7

The Global Diet

READING SKILL

- Skimming, page 149

VOCABULARY STRATEGIES

- Understanding Demonstrative Pronouns, page 146
- Understanding Vocabulary in Context—Parallel Clauses, page 153

GRAPHICS

- Understanding Diagrams, page 156

Answer the questions and briefly discuss your answers with a partner.

1. Do you think you have a healthful diet?
2. What is considered a healthful diet in your family?
3. Look at the photos. What health risks or benefits, if any, do you think may be associated with eating any of these foods or food products?

a

b

c

The Global Diet | 141

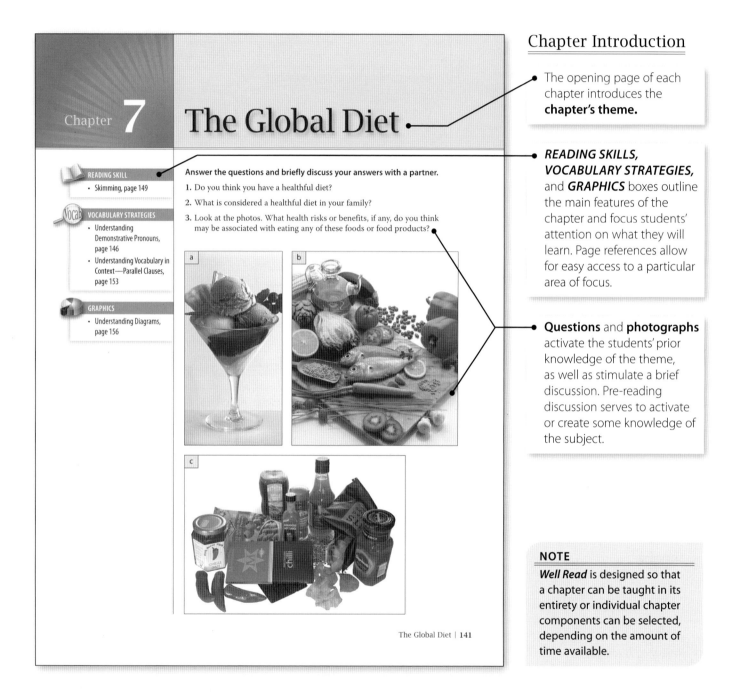

Chapter Introduction

- The opening page of each chapter introduces the **chapter's theme.**
- ***READING SKILLS, VOCABULARY STRATEGIES,*** and ***GRAPHICS*** boxes outline the main features of the chapter and focus students' attention on what they will learn. Page references allow for easy access to a particular area of focus.
- **Questions** and **photographs** activate the students' prior knowledge of the theme, as well as stimulate a brief discussion. Pre-reading discussion serves to activate or create some knowledge of the subject.

NOTE

Well Read is designed so that a chapter can be taught in its entirety or individual chapter components can be selected, depending on the amount of time available.

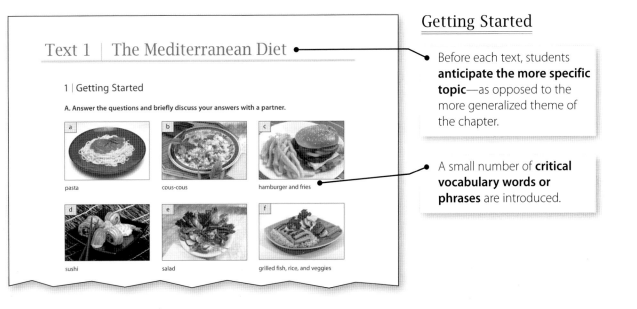

Before each text, students **anticipate the more specific topic**—as opposed to the more generalized theme of the chapter.

A small number of **critical vocabulary words or phrases** are introduced.

Active Previewing and Skimming

Students are taught how to *actively* **preview** a wide range of genres, both academic and non-academic, including newspaper articles, online texts, magazine articles, textbook articles, and graphics (see **Graphics** on page xii).

The skill of **skimming** a text for general meaning is also introduced in later chapters, at which point, there is no need to do a separate preview of a text.

Text 1 | The Mediterranean Diet

1 | Getting Started

A. Answer the questions and briefly discuss your answers with a partner.

- a — pasta
- b — cous-cous
- c — hamburger and fries
- d — sushi
- e — salad
- f — grilled fish, rice, and veggies

---

2 | Active Previewing

A. Preview the newspaper article below by reading the first two paragraphs. Then with a partner, answer as much as you can without looking at the text.

1. Whom (what group of people) is this article about?
2. What are they doing?
3. Where are they from?

B. Work as a class or in large groups. Try to name as many things as you can about the text.

C. Answer the questions with a partner.

1. What is the topic of this text?
2. What is the main idea of this text?

3 | Reading and Recalling

A. Read the text. Stop after each subtitled section and tell a partner two things that you remember about it.

---

2 | Skimming

Skim the online article on the next page in five minutes or less. Then answer the questions with a partner.

1. Are chili peppers a fruit or a vegetable?
2. What is capsicum?
3. Where were chili peppers first cultivated?
4. What are three places, regions, or countries mentioned in the article that use chili peppers in their cuisines?
5. What is one medical benefit offered by chili peppers?

B. Work as a class or in large groups. Try to name as many things as you can about the text.

C. Answer the questions with a partner.

1. What is the topic of this text?
2. What is the main idea of this text?

> **REMINDER**
> Skim the text by reading the title, the introduction, the first paragraph, the first sentence of each paragraph, the final paragraph of the text, and by looking at the photograph and the caption. Note names, places, and dates.
> For more on *skimming*, see page 149.

Text 1, 2, and 4

The **texts** progress in length and level of difficulty in each chapter, and they are **authentic** in both presentation and content. Genres include: online texts, newspaper articles, magazine articles, and textbook articles, among others.

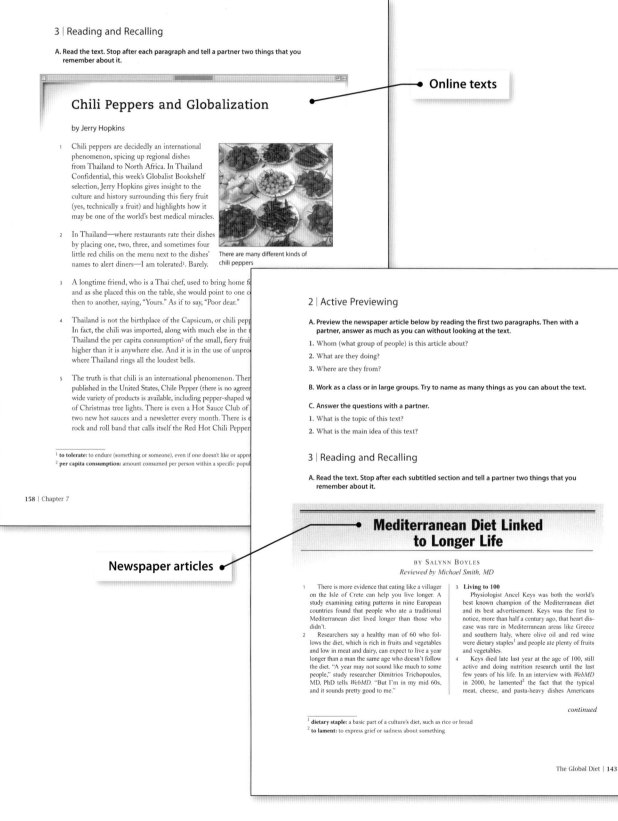

3 | Reading and Recalling

A. Read the text. Stop after each paragraph and tell a partner two things that you remember about it.

Chili Peppers and Globalization

by Jerry Hopkins

1 Chili peppers are decidedly an international phenomenon, spicing up regional dishes from Thailand to North Africa. In Thailand Confidential, this week's Globalist Bookshelf selection, Jerry Hopkins gives insight to the culture and history surrounding this fiery fruit (yes, technically a fruit) and highlights how it may be one of the world's best medical miracles.

2 In Thailand—where restaurants rate their dishes by placing one, two, three, and sometimes four little red chilis on the menu next to the dishes' names to alert diners—I am tolerated[1]. Barely.

There are many different kinds of chili peppers

3 A longtime friend, who is a Thai chef, used to bring home f[...] and as she placed this on the table, she would point to one c[...] then to another, saying, "Yours." As if to say, "Poor dear."

4 Thailand is not the birthplace of the Capsicum, or chili pepp[...] In fact, the chili was imported, along with much else in the [...] Thailand the per capita consumption[2] of the small, fiery frui[...] higher than it is anywhere else. And it is in the use of unpro[...] where Thailand rings all the loudest bells.

5 The truth is that chili is an international phenomenon. Ther[...] published in the United States, Chile Pepper (there is no agree[...] wide variety of products is available, including pepper-shaped w[...] of Christmas tree lights. There is even a Hot Sauce Club of [...] two new hot sauces and a newsletter every month. There is e[...] rock and roll band that calls itself the Red Hot Chili Pepper[...]

---

[1] **to tolerate:** to endure (something or someone), even if one doesn't like or appre[...]
[2] **per capita consumption:** amount consumed per person within a specific popul[...]

158 | Chapter 7

Online texts

Newspaper articles

2 | Active Previewing

A. Preview the newspaper article below by reading the first two paragraphs. Then with a partner, answer as much as you can without looking at the text.

1. Whom (what group of people) is this article about?
2. What are they doing?
3. Where are they from?

B. Work as a class or in large groups. Try to name as many things as you can about the text.

C. Answer the questions with a partner.

1. What is the topic of this text?
2. What is the main idea of this text?

3 | Reading and Recalling

A. Read the text. Stop after each subtitled section and tell a partner two things that you remember about it.

Mediterranean Diet Linked to Longer Life

BY SALYNN BOYLES
Reviewed by Michael Smith, MD

1 There is more evidence that eating like a villager on the Isle of Crete can help you live longer. A study examining eating patterns in nine European countries found that people who ate a traditional Mediterranean diet lived longer than those who didn't.

2 Researchers say a healthy man of 60 who follows the diet, which is rich in fruits and vegetables and low in meat and dairy, can expect to live a year longer than a man the same age who doesn't follow the diet. "A year may not sound like much to some people," study researcher Dimitrios Trichopoulos, MD, PhD tells *WebMD*. "But I'm in my mid 60s, and it sounds pretty good to me."

3 **Living to 100**
Physiologist Ancel Keys was both the world's best known champion of the Mediterranean diet and its best advertisement. Keys was the first to notice, more than half a century ago, that heart disease was rare in Mediterranean areas like Greece and southern Italy, where olive oil and red wine were dietary staples[1] and people ate plenty of fruits and vegetables.

4 Keys died late last year at the age of 100, still active and doing nutrition research until the last few years of his life. In an interview with *WebMD* in 2000, he lamented[2] the fact that the typical meat, cheese, and pasta-heavy dishes Americans

continued

---

[1] **dietary staple:** a basic part of a culture's diet, such as rice or bread
[2] **to lament:** to express grief or sadness about something

The Global Diet | 143

C. Answer the questions with a partner.

1. What is the topic of this text?

2. What is the main idea of this text?

3 | Reading and Recalling

A. Read the text. Stop after each paragraph and tell a partner two things that you remember about it.

Soy: It Does a Body Good
BY PSYCHOLOGY TODAY STAFF

1   Eating soy, it now appears, is one of the simplest things we can do to boost[1] our health. Once revered as a sacred crop in China, soybeans are one of the richest plant sources of protein. In fact, the World Health Organization considers it on a par with meat and dairy proteins. And not only is this low-fat dietary protein great news for vegetarians or dieters, but a growing body of research also indicates that soy may help prevent many chronic diseases.

2   Many of soy's therapeutic benefits are believed to come from its vast stores[2] of bioactive plant chemicals called isoflavones. These are able to stabilize estrogen, a female hormone necessary for normal growth and development. They adjust the hormone's effects when levels are too high or low.

3   To get the most out of soy, health experts suggest eating whole foods like tofu, soymilk, and tempeh because they contain higher levels of isoflavones than supplements[3] do. Fortunately, there are now a variety of soy and tofu products that are both convenient and tasty. Both fresh and long-conservation soymilk are easy to find in many supermarkets, and soymilk can be used in place of cow's milk for both drinking and cooking.

4   The biggest news is that soy reduces cholesterol and protects against heart disease. This was demonstrated in an analysis of 38 studies published in the prestigious *New England Journal of Medicine*. The analysis showed that eating soy lowers total levels of cholesterol by 10% and LDL or "bad" cholesterol by 13%. In 1999, the Food

Tofu, soy sauce, and soy milk are just some of the products made with soy.

and Drug Administration gave soy the green light, stating definitively that eating 25 grams of soy protein each day as part of a low-fat, low-cholesterol diet reduces the risk of heart disease. Recently, the American Heart Association revised its dietary guidelines to recommend soy as part of a heart-healthy diet.

5   While research on othe[...] clusive, scientists believe t[...] protect against osteoporos[...]

---
[1] **to boost:** to increase; to assist in the progress of; to better
[2] **store:** great number or quantity; supply
[3] **supplement:** something that is added to complete something else that has a lack; here: vitamin, mineral, enzyme, etc. that would be taken to fulfill a nutritional lack

Magazine articles

2 | Active Previewing

A. Preview the academic text below and tell a partner two things you remember about it.

B. Work as a class or in large groups. Try to say as many things as you can about the text.

C. Answer the questions with a partner.

1. What is the topic of this text?

2. What is the main idea of this text?

> **REMEMBER**
> Preview academic texts by reading the title, the subtitles, the first sentence of each paragraph, and the final sentence of the text. Preview longer academic texts a second time.
> For more about *previewing academic texts*, see page 3.

3 | Reading and Recalling

A. Read the text. Stop after each paragraph and tell a partner two things that you remember about it.

Textbook articles

Putting on a New Face
The Creation of a Caring Corporation

by Cynthia Kersey

1   No one who has ever followed a dream has taken a direct path and arrived at his or her destination effortlessly and on time. Following a dream can be a bumpy road full of twists and turns and occasional roadblocks. The journey requires changes and adjustments in both thought and action, not just once, but over and over. Anita Roddick, the founder of The Body Shop®, used creativity to overcome challenges that would have stopped the vast majority of new business owners. She broke just about every rule of business when she started The Body Shop®, and she continued to break the rules until she recently retired.

2   Of course, such irreverence[1] has its consequences. In Anita's case, the consequences read like this: The Body Shop® now has more than 1,500 stores around the world, is worth over $500

million, and has influenced the products and marketing of all its major competitors. And those are just the consequences in the business arena. The Body Shop® is also a powerfully effective vehicle for social and environmental awareness and change; as far as Anita is concerned, that is the most important consequence of all.

3   From the moment in 1976 when Anita first conceived the idea of opening a shop to sell naturally based cosmetics, she was thinking in a most unbusinesslike manner. Most entrepreneurs set out to create a company with growth potential that will make them wealthy someday. Anita was just looking for a way to feed herself and her two children, while her husband, also a maverick[2], was away on a two-year adventure, riding a horse from Argentina to New York.

4   Anita's first challenge was to find a cosmetics manufacturer to produce her products. No one she approached had ever heard of jojoba oil or aloe vera gel, and they all thought that cocoa butter had something to do with chocolate. Although she didn't realize it at the time, Anita had discovered a market that was just about to explode: young female consumers who would prefer their cosmetics to be produced in a

continued

---
[1] **irreverence:** disrespect
[2] **maverick:** a person who resists the regular rules of society

Understanding the Text

4 | Understanding the Text

A. Answer as many questions as you can without looking at the text. Discuss your answers with a partner.

1. What did Ancel Keyes think about the Mediterranean diet? _____

2. What is a "Mediterranean diet"? _____

3. What did the results of the study in Europe show? _____
_____

B. Complete the chart according to the text. Discuss your answers with a partner.

People who follow a traditional Mediterranean diet...
1. eat mostly plant foods (fruits, vegetables, beans, whole grains, nuts, etc.).
2.
3.
4.

5 | Understanding the Topic and Main Idea

Text. Answer the questions and discuss your answers with a partner.

1. What is the topic of the text? _____

2. What is the main idea of the text? _____
_____

3. Are your answers for the topic and the main idea here the same as the ones you determined after you previewed the text, or are your answers different? _____

8 | Reading Critically—Facts, Opinions, and Inferences

Write F for Fact, O for Opinion, or I for Inference according to the text. Discuss your answers with a partner.

__F__ 1. A study found that people who ate a traditional Mediterranean diet lived longer than those who didn't.

_____ 2. Ancel Keys was the world's best known champion of the Mediterranean diet.

_____ 3. Keys wished the food served in American-Italian restaurants were more like traditional Mediterranean fare.

_____ 4. Low-carbohydrate diets are not the most healthful diets.

_____ 5. Two-thirds of Americans are overweight or obese.

9 | Discussing the Issues

Answer the questions and discuss your answers with a partner.

1. Would you change the way you eat in order to have better health? Why or why not?

2. How do you think this text might persuade someone to make any changes in his or her diet?

3. In your opinion, what is the best way to stay healthy?

Understanding the Text

After each text, students are presented with a **two-part reading comprehension activity**. The first part checks the students' comprehension of the most basic ideas expressed in the text, whereas the second part challenges the students to recall other key ideas and information. Students are asked to complete as much as they can without looking back at the text.

Understanding the Topic, Main Idea, and Supporting Details

Topic, Main Idea, and *Supporting Details* are introduced in separate chapters, allowing for **practice and mastery** before progressing to the next skill. Earlier chapters present choices in a **multiple choice format**, whereas subsequent chapters require the students to **write their own interpretations**.

Practice Activities

A variety of activities allow students to practice the reading skills and vocabulary strategies, allowing for **recycling, review, and mastery**. (see *Reading Skills* and *Vocabulary Strategies* on page xi).

Discussing the Issues

Every text ends with a series of questions that encourage the students to **express their opinions and ideas** about the general subject discussed in the text.

Reading Skills

READING SKILL Skimming

Skimming is letting your eyes glide through a text as you read quickly. A reader **skims** a text when he or she wants to get a general idea about the information contained in the text but does not need to know full details.

For example, skimming is useful when a reader:

a. wants to see if the full text is worth reading.

b. wants to find key facts about a subject.

c. wants to know the outcome or status of a current event.

d. is writing a term paper and has to look through dozens of sources for useful information.

e. wants to know which movies or restaurants the local newspaper recommends and why.

f. has only a few minutes to review a business report before a meeting.

g. is reading a story and cannot wait to find out what happens in the end.

To skim:

1. Read the title and any subtitles.

2. Read the first one or two paragraphs.

3. Read the first and/or last sentence of the other paragraphs.

4. Look quickly over the body of the other paragraphs, reading only a few words here and there. You may note names, places, dates and numbers, and words in bold or italic print.

5. Read the last paragraph.

2 | Skimming

A. Skim the magazine article on the next page in three minutes or less. Then answer the questions with a partner.

1. Acco... healt...

2. Wha...

3. Wha...

4. How...

5. In wh...

B. Work...

- The first two texts in each chapter introduce students to **new reading skills** and **vocabulary strategies.** They are always followed by a practice activity.

- Text 4, a more academic text, **incorporates all of the skills** and **strategies** taught in Text 1 and Text 2, as well as selected skills and strategies taught in previous chapters.

- The reading skills include *Active Previewing, Skimming, Scanning, Making Inferences,* and *Understanding the Topic, Main Idea,* and *Supporting Details,* among others.

Vocabulary Strategies

VOCABULARY STRATEGY Understanding Demonstrative Pronouns

Demonstrative pronouns point to and identify nouns or pronouns. They can function as subjects, objects, or objects of a preposition. The singular demonstrative pronouns are **this** and **that**, and the plural demonstrative pronouns are **these** and **those**.

Read the following sentences.

1. You can't point to one thing and say *that* is what does it. (¶7)

The demonstrative pronoun *that* refers to the noun phrase *one thing.* In other words, the first sentence could read: "You can't point to one thing and say the one thing is what does it."

Note: Do not confuse demonstrative pronouns with adjectives. Adjectives modify nouns, whereas demonstrative pronouns *represent* or *replace* the nouns. Read the sentence.

2. In *this* case, the total is better than the sum of the parts..." (¶7)

This is an adjective that modifies the noun *case.*

6 | Understanding Demonstrative Pronouns

Write what each demonstrative pronoun refers to according to the text.

1. those (those who didn't) (¶1) _____

2. that (there is more to it than that) (¶7) _____

3. that (that is still not clear) (¶7) _____

7 | Understanding Vocabulary in Context—Context Clues

Select the best meaning for each word or phrase according to the text.

1. sparingly (¶7)
   a. in equal amounts   b. in large amounts   c. in small amounts

2. in moderation (¶7)
   a. in limited amounts   b. a lot   c. never

3. refined (¶7)
   a. derived from plants   b. artificially purified   c. natural

- Students are introduced to a variety of vocabulary strategies that can help them determine the meanings of new vocabulary **without using their dictionaries**.

- Students also learn how to recognize pronouns and possessive adjectives, as well as how to **make logical assumptions** about their referents.

- All vocabulary strategies present the vocabulary as it is used in the texts themselves, **in context**, yet the strategies themselves **can be applied universally** to reading that students do outside class.

Graphics

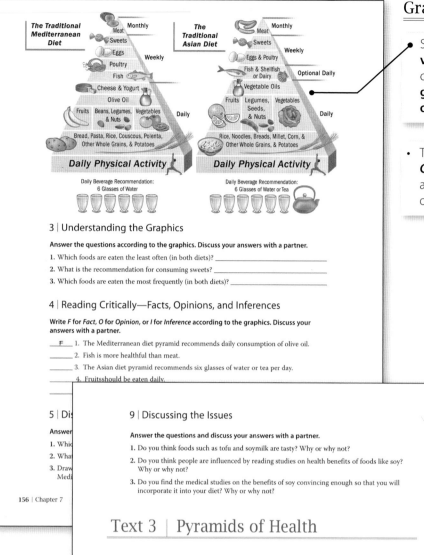

Students are exposed to a **variety of graphics**. Text 3 of each chapter is always a **graphical representation on the chapter's theme**.

- The graphics include *Tables, Charts, Graphs, Timelines,* and *Illustrations,* among others.

3 | Understanding the Graphics

Answer the questions according to the graphics. Discuss your answers with a partner.

1. Which foods are eaten the least often (in both diets)? _____
2. What is the recommendation for consuming sweets? _____
3. Which foods are eaten the most frequently (in both diets)? _____

4 | Reading Critically—Facts, Opinions, and Inferences

Write *F* for *Fact*, *O* for *Opinion*, or *I* for *Inference* according to the graphics. Discuss your answers with a partner.

___F___ 1. The Mediterranean diet pyramid recommends daily consumption of olive oil.

_____ 2. Fish is more healthful than meat.

_____ 3. The Asian diet pyramid recommends six glasses of water or tea per day.

_____ 4. Fruitsshould be eaten daily.

5 | Dis

Answer

1. Whic
2. Wha
3. Draw
   Medi

---

9 | Discussing the Issues

Answer the questions and discuss your answers with a partner.

1. Do you think foods such as tofu and soymilk are tasty? Why or why not?
2. Do you think people are influenced by reading studies on health benefits of foods like soy? Why or why not?
3. Do you find the medical studies on the benefits of soy convincing enough so that you will incorporate it into your diet? Why or why not?

Text 3 | Pyramids of Health

1 | Getting Started

Complete the chart and then briefly discuss your answers with a partner.

I eat . . .	Monthly	Weekly	Daily	Never
bread, rice, noodles, or pasta	☐	☐	☐	☐
eggs	☐	☐	☐	☐
fish or shellfish	☐	☐	☐	☐
fruits and vegetables	☐	☐	☐	☐
meat (beef, pork, lamb, etc.)	☐	☐	☐	☐
poultry (chicken, turkey, duck, goose, etc.)	☐	☐	☐	☐
sweets (candy, pastries, cakes, ice cream, etc.)	☐	☐	☐	☐

2 | Active Previewing

Preview the diagrams on the next page and then answer the questions with a partner.

1. What regions are represented by the diagrams?
2. What is the topic of these diagrams?

> **REMINDER**
> Preview diagrams by reading the title, the subtitles, and then by looking at the diagrams as a whole.
> For more on *previewing diagrams*, see page 130.

NOTE

Throughout *Well Read*, help is provided in the margin. *Remember, Note,* and *Online Tip* boxes give suggestions and page references to aid students as they work.

Putting It On Paper

A. Write a five-paragraph essay on one of these topics.

1. A friend or relative wants to improve his or her diet for health reasons and asks you to help create a gradual plan for more healthful nutrition. Describe the process you will recommend.

2. Describe how a food, a food product, or a food style—such as vegetarianism or fast food—might gradually become popular.

Steps for your essay

a. In your first paragraph, clearly state your recommendation or opinion about your topic and your general reason or reasons why.

b. Your second, third, and fourth paragraphs should each contain a different reason that supports your topic.

c. In your final paragraph, summarize the ideas you state in your essay.

B. Exchange essays with a partner. First, read your partner's essay and answer the questions on the checklist. Then give feedback to your partner.

> **NOTE**
> Each of your paragraphs should contain a main idea that is supported by details—facts, data, examples, etc.—that prove or illustrate your main idea. For more on *supporting details*, see page 77.

✔ CHECKLIST

1. Does ¶1 show your partner's recommendation or opinion about the topic?
2. Do the three body paragraphs support the topic?
3. Does the final paragraph summarize the ideas contained in the essay?
4. Does each paragraph contain a main idea?
5. Do the details of each paragraph support the main idea?
6. Are you persuaded by your partner's recommendation or opinion?
7. Is there any information in the essay that is not related to your partner's thesis? If yes, please underline it on your partner's essay, and write it below:

C. Revis

Putting It On Paper

- In each chapter, students have the opportunity to write a **paragraph, letter**, or **essay** based on the chapter's theme.

- The writing activity complements the chapter texts, yet it is also **designed to stand independently** if all of the chapter texts are not covered.

- Each *Putting It On Paper* activity offers **two writing prompts**.

Taking It Online | Food and More Food

A. With a partner, use the Internet to research healthful and unhealthful foods.

1. Use Google (www.google.com) or another major search engine to begin your online research.

2. Search for websites with information about two foods that are believed to be good for long-term health and two foods that aren't. In addition to the food name, these words may be helpful in your search:

food

health benefit

health risk

beneficial

damaging

healthful

3. Preview the websites.

> **ONLINE TIP**
> Many large websites have their own search engines. Use these search engines to help save time when looking for information related to your search.

B. Complete the table with the information you find.

Healthful Foods	
Food:	Food:
Website:	Website:
Benefit:	Benefit:

Unhealthful Foods	
Food:	Food:
Website:	Website:
Benefit:	Benefit:

C. **Following up.** In small groups, discuss your eating habits. Think of three ways you could use the information you found on the Internet to improve your own diet.

Taking It Online

- Every chapter culminates with a *Taking It Online* activity. This activity guides students through the steps necessary for **conducting online research**, based on the theme of the chapter.

- The online activity is **open** to the extent that students are encouraged to find their own sites, **but it is also focused** enough so that students will not be roaming through undirected data.

- *Taking It Online* finishes with a **follow-up activity** that enables students to **take their research one step further**, in pairs or groups.

Reflecting on Film

Answer the questions and briefly discuss your answers with a partner.

1. Do you like to watch foreign language movies?

2. Look at the photos. Where are these movies being made?

3. What countries are famous for movie-making?

Text 1 | Hollywood Dreams

1 | Getting Started

A. Answer the questions and briefly discuss your answers with a partner.

1. Do you ever go to the movies?

2. Where do you think the first movies were made?

3. Do you think that people go to the movies as often today as they did 25 years ago?

4. Would you prefer to go to the movies or watch television? Why?

5. How do movie-making companies make money today?

B. Check (✔) whether you think movie production would go up or down as a result of major events. Briefly discuss your answers with a partner.

Major Events	Movie Production ↑	Movie Production ↓
1. the invention of television	☐	☐
2. a big war	☐	☐
3. a serious financial crisis	☐	☐

VOCABULARY STRATEGY Skipping Words and Phrases

When reading a text, you may encounter unfamiliar words or phrases. One good strategy is to **skip them.** They may not be necessary to understand the meaning of a paragraph or the meaning of the whole text.

However, if you find that a paragraph is unclear when you skip words or phrases,

1. Figure out the part of speech of the words or phrases you skipped (noun, adjective, verb, adverb).

2. Think about what you understand.

3. Keep reading.

Read the following sentence.

Hollywood rushed to fill the **void**, and film-making became a major industry. (¶3)

Imagine you do not understand the bolded word. Ask yourself: What did Hollywood rush to fill? The article *the* suggests that the skipped word is a noun: *Hollywood rushed to fill the* "something," *and film-making became a major industry.* Think about what you do understand: We know that film-making became a major industry when Hollywood rushed to fill the "something." At this point, we have enough information to keep reading.

2 | Skipping Words and Phrases

A. Read the following sentences. Write the parts of speech of the missing words.

1. Hollywood did not become the xxxxxx picture capital of the United States until nearly twenty years after the invention of movies. _____

2. From these xxxxxx beginnings, movies soon became a national art form. _____

3. Producers decided to make their financial position more solid by xxxxxxxxx large chains of theaters. _____

4. To maintain audience interest, studios produced a range of xxxxxx, including musicals, comedies, and westerns. _____

5. The major Hollywood companies have become huge entertainment xxxxxxxxxxxx with interests in recorded music, television programming, book publishing, and cable communications in all the xxxxxxxxx world markets. _____

B. With a partner, discuss what you do understand about each sentence.

> **READING SKILL** Previewing Online Articles, Magazine Articles, and Academic Texts
>
> **Previewing** will give you a general idea of what a text is about. To preview online articles, magazine articles, and academic texts:
>
> 1. Read the title and any subtitles.
>
> 2. Look at any photos, graphs, or charts.
>
> 3. Read the first sentence of each paragraph.
>
> 4. Read the last sentence of the text.

3 | Active Previewing

Preview the online article on the next page. Underline the title, the first sentence of each paragraph, and the last sentence of the text as you preview. Then answer this question with a partner.

What do you think this text is about?

4 | Reading and Recalling

A. Read the text. Stop after each paragraph and tell a partner two things that you remember about it.

The Dream Factory

by Tino Balio

1   Hollywood did not become the motion picture capital of the United States until nearly twenty years after the invention of movies. Production was centered in the New York City area from 1894, when Thomas Edison introduced his Kinetoscope[1], until 1908, when American producers began moving to southern California to take advantage of the temperate climate and varied scenery to produce films year-round. Most early movie patrons were immigrant workers and their families in search of cheap entertainment.

REMEMBER

Skip the words and phrases that you do not understand.

2   From these humble beginnings, movies soon became a national art form. Two developments encouraged the transition: feature films and the "star" system. The growth of motion pictures from short, fifteen-minute films to features lasting 90 minutes and longer made it possible to tell complex stories that could compete with the theater. New motion picture stars such as Mary Pickford, Charles Chaplin, and Douglas Fairbanks created fans who, by buying tickets, supported the high salaries paid to these stars.

3   Hollywood was only one of several players in the world film market until the First World War, when film production in Europe almost came to a stop. Hollywood rushed to fill the void, and film-making became a major industry. Producers decided to make their financial position more solid by acquiring large chains of theaters; these theaters needed a steady supply of films. After the invention of movies with sound—called "talkies"—in 1926, only the strongest film companies had the financial resources to make the conversion to sound. The result was that by 1930, eight companies virtually dominated Hollywood, and most of these continue to dominate the business to this day: Loew's (MGM®), Paramount®, Warner Bros.®, Twentieth Century-Fox®, RKO®, Universal®, Columbia®, and United Artists®.

4   Hollywood reached the height of its influence during the 1930s and 1940s. After a brief decline during the Great Depression, movie theater attendance in the United States rose steadily until it reached nearly 80 million a week by 1946. This figure nearly equaled the entire population of the country.

continued

---

[1] **Kinetoscope:** the machine that came before the modern movie projector

continued

5   To keep cinemas well stocked with films, Hollywood had perfected an efficient form of mass production. Studios were organized by departments, such as screen-writing, editing, and sound, all headed by a production chief who oversaw operations. The major studios turned out two types of pictures: class A, with big-name stars and big budgets, and class B, economy films. To maintain audience interest, studios produced a range of genres, including musicals, comedies, and westerns. And to satisfy motion picture censors[2], the industry adopted the Motion Picture Production Code in 1930, whereby producers voluntarily agreed to make their film content follow a generally accepted code.

6   After the Second World War, a series of problems forced Hollywood companies to drastically change their operations. One problem was that in 1948 the U.S. Supreme Court charged the major companies with having violated antitrust laws[3] and forced them to sell off their profitable motion picture theaters and to end restrictive trade practices. Soon after, the rise of television caused movie theater attendance to drop by 50 percent during the 1950s. Furthermore, Hollywood had problems selling films overseas. Before the war, Europe had been the largest overseas market for American films. After the war, however, nations worked to rebuild their economies and contributed more to their own film industries.

7   Hollywood responded to these conditions by producing fewer pictures and cutting jobs, by making movies in color to compete with television, and by producing pictures abroad to take advantage of government subsidies[4]. In addition, the big Hollywood companies recognized that television offered new distribution potential, and invested in it accordingly. These measures revived Hollywood and helped establish its crucial role in the multi-media entertainment industry of today. Now, the major Hollywood companies are huge entertainment conglomerates[5] with interests in recorded music, television programming, book publishing, and cable communications in all the principal world markets. Hollywood is the motion-picture capital of the world, and it will remain so by strengthening its partnerships with foreign interests.

_____

[2] **censor:** a person who is authorized to examine films or other media in order to remove unacceptable material

[3] **antitrust laws:** state and federal laws protecting individuals and businesses from monopolies and unfair restrictions

[4] **government subsidies:** financial assistance from the government

[5] **conglomerate:** a large corporation or business that operates in many industries—usually unrelated to each other

B. Read the text again without pausing. Tell your partner two new pieces of information that you remember.

C. Work as a class or in large groups. Try to name as many things as you can about the text.

5 | Understanding the Text

A. Look at the photos and then answer the question without looking at the text. Discuss your answer with a partner.

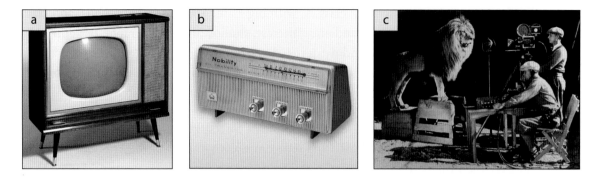

Which photo best accompanies the text on pages 4 and 5? Why?

_____

_____

B. Answer as many questions as you can without looking at the text. Discuss your answers with a partner.

1. Why did the center of movie production move from New York City to Hollywood in 1908?

   a. Thomas Edison introduced the Kinetoscope.

   b. Producers wanted to take advantage of the climate and scenery.

   c. Immigrant families wanted cheap entertainment.

2. What allowed movies to become a national art form?

   a. television

   b. feature films and the star system

   c. high salaries

3. How popular were movies in the 1930s and 40s?

   a. very popular

   b. not very popular

   c. moderately popular

4. What was one problem that Hollywood encountered after the Second World War?

   a. Eight companies dominated Hollywood.

   b. New motion picture stars were paid high salaries.

   c. Television caused movie theater attendance to drop.

6 | Discussing the Issues

Answer the questions and discuss your answers with a partner.

1. What are the advantages of going to see a movie over watching a movie on television? What are the advantages of watching television over going to see a movie?

2. Why is this text titled *The Dream Factory?*

3. Which three film genres are most popular? Why?

Text 2 | A Movie Close to Home

1 | Getting Started

A. Answer the questions and briefly discuss your answers with a partner.

1. Have you ever seen a movie from another culture?

2. Is it important for movie-goers to see movies from different cultures? Why or why not?

3. What can we learn from foreign movies?

B. Check (✔) whether you agree or disagree. Briefly discuss your answers with a partner.

Movies should ...	Agree	Disagree
1. ... be interesting to a wide variety of movie-goers.	☐	☐
2. ... show human relationships.	☐	☐
3. ... discuss history or current events.	☐	☐
4. ... teach movie-goers about other cultures or countries.	☐	☐
5. ... include characters from a variety of backgrounds.	☐	☐

2 | Skipping Words and Phrases

A. Read the following sentences. First, cross out the words and phrases you do not understand. Then write their parts of speech on the blanks.

1. The travails of Raz, a young Arab American woman searching for her true self, are the theme of a feature film that producers hope to shoot in Jordan with the western market as its target audience. _____

2. The film, *Falls the Shadow,* is the brainchild of Jackie Oweis Sawiris, an Arab American director born of a Jordanian mother and Egyptian father. _____

3. The objective is to show that the Middle East is not only about politics and religion; it is also home to a deep-rooted culture that is being ignored. _____

4. The film could act as a prototype upon which other Jordanian film productions could be based. _____

5. One of those who have expressed interest in taking a leading role in the film is the renowned Moroccan actor Said Taghmaoui. _____

B. With a partner, discuss what you do understand about each sentence.

3 | Active Previewing

Preview the magazine article below. Underline the title, the first sentence of each paragraph, and the last sentence of the text as you preview. Then answer these questions with a partner.

1. What are some of the countries mentioned?

2. What do you think this text is about?

4 | Reading and Recalling

A. Read the text. Stop after each paragraph and tell a partner two things that you remember about it.

Director Envisions Her Film as Prototype for Jordanian Cinema

BY NATASHA TWAL TYNES

1   The travails of Raz, a young Arab American woman searching for her true self, are the theme of a feature film that producers hope to shoot entirely in Jordan with the western market as its target audience.

2   The film, *Falls the Shadow*, is the brainchild of Jackie Oweis Sawiris, an Arab American director born of a Jordanian mother and Egyptian father. The film project "is a semi-autobiographical[1] epic love story of denial, the search for and, ultimately, the acceptance of self," explained Sawiris, also a screenwriter and an actress.

> The film is also about breaking stereotypes.

3   For the enthusiastic 39-year-old director, the project is not just about making a movie. The film is also about breaking stereotypes. "The objective is to show that the Middle East is not only about politics and religion; it is also home to a deep-rooted culture that is being ignored," Sawiris told *The Jordan Times*, explaining that Jordan is the primary focus of the project.

4   Sawiris believes the film could help the burgeoning[2] Jordanian film industry to be able to take part in the international film community. It could act as a prototype upon which other Jordanian film productions could be based.

5   Furthermore, Sawiris, who admits to rebelling at an early age against her origins and her "curly black hair," believes it is the responsibility of Arab Americans to change the image of Arabs in the U.S. "My way of doing that is by making movies, as I believe showing is more effective than telling." According to the filmmaker, the Kingdom of Jordan needs to improve its image, which can be done through movies.

continued

---

[1] **semi-autobiographical: semi:** partial; **autobiography:** an account about a person's life written by that person

[2] **to burgeon:** to begin to grow

continued

6   The locations for Sawiris's film are all over the country, in Amman, Aqaba, the Dead Sea, Wadi Rum, and Petra. "The tourist benefit is a well-known added bonus of making a film on location," says Sawiris. She noted the increase in popularity of Thailand and London after the movies *The Beach* and *Notting Hill* were released. "I want people who watch it in places like Times Square or Leicester Square to say: 'What a cool place. I want to go there.'"

7   Also an actress, Sawiris considers her nanny role in Stanley Kubrick's *Eyes Wide Shut* as her major achievement. "I feel fortunate that I got to work with such a brilliant person before he passed away," said Sawiris, who holds a bachelor's degree in journalism from New York University. "He encouraged me to continue with acting, as I was about to give up from sheer frustration."

8   Sawiris was in search of funding for the ambitious project in Jordan. Her contacts within the industry in the U.S. and U.K. allowed her to bring together a professional team from both the Middle East and the West. Sawiris is teaming up with Netherlands-based Jordanian director

Mahmoud Massad, whose movie *Shatter Hassan* gained a number of international awards. And one of those who have expressed interest in taking a leading role in the film is renowned[3] Moroccan actor Said Taghmaoui. He played in *Three Kings* with George Clooney and in *Hideous Kinky* with Kate Winslet.

9   Two of the leading characters will come from the West, while the remainder will be drawn from the Arab world—primarily Jordan, said the director. "Just as the story of *Falls the Shadow* unites the Western and the Middle Eastern worlds, so will the production itself." The film's protagonists[4] are Sevrin, a spiritual being waiting to reunite with the woman he lost, Zayna, a mother searching for the child taken away from her, Raz, the American returning to a country she rejected, and Zeid, a man falling out of love with his homeland and in love with Raz.

10   For Sawiris, the heart of the movie is Jordan itself. "I got offers to do the same script in Mexico and in India," she says, "But I turned them down.[5] The movie is entirely about the country I fell in love with."

___

[3] **renowned:** famous
[4] **protagonist:** the main character in a book, play, or film
[5] **to turn down:** to refuse

B. Read the text again without pausing. Tell your partner two new pieces of information that you remember.

C. Work as a class or in large groups. Try to name as many things as you can about the text.

5 | Understanding the Text

A. Answer as many questions as you can without looking at the text. Discuss your answers with a partner.

1. Who is Jackie Oweis Sawiris?

   a. an Arab American woman searching for her true self

   b. a Jordanian mother

   c. an Arab American director

2. What does Sawiris want to do?

   a. find her daughter

   b. make a movie

   c. star in a movie

3. What is one way in which Sawiris plans to unite the Western and Middle Eastern worlds through her project?

   a. by starring in the film herself

   b. through the story line of the film, as well as the actors

   c. by shooting the film in the West with only Middle Eastern actors

B. Check (✔) the correct answers according to the text. Discuss your answers with a partner.

She ...	Jackie	Raz
1. ... is searching for her true self.		
2. ... has a Jordanian mother and an Egyptian father.		
3. ... rebelled at an early age against her curly black hair.		
4. ... is looking for funding in Jordan.		
5. ... is returning to the country she rejected.		

6 | Discussing the Issues

Answer the questions and discuss your answers with a partner.

1. According to Sawiris, showing is better than telling. Do you agree or disagree with this statement? Why?

2. Do you think the fact that Sawiris is a woman will be more of an advantage or a disadvantage for getting her film produced? Why?

3. Do you think that movies can change people's opinions or ideas about a culture or country? Why or why not?

Text 3 | At the Movies

1 | Getting Started

Answer the questions and briefly discuss your answers with a partner.

1. Is there a movie theater in your city or town?

2. How often do you go to the movies?

3. Do you think that there are more or fewer movie theaters today than there were 20 years ago? Why?

> **GRAPHICS** Understanding Tables
>
> **Tables** are used to present numerical or statistical information. **Preview** tables by reading the title, the column and/or row headers and any **boldfaced** or *italicized* information.

2 | Active Previewing

Preview the table below, and then answer the questions. Discuss your answers with a partner.

1. What is the title of this table?

2. What is this table about?

   a. the average movie ticket price in the U.S.

   b. the U.S. motion picture industry

   c. the motion picture industry

U.S. MOTION PICTURE INDUSTRY OVERVIEW							
			ADMISSIONS (#)		TOTAL TICKET SALES ($)		
Year	New Pictures Released	Number of Indoor Screens	Total in Millions	Per Screen*	In Millions	Per Screen	Avg. Ticket Price
1980	193	14,171	1,021.50	72,084	$2,749	$193,988	$2.69
1985	389	18,327	1,056.00	57,620	$3,749	$204,562	$3.55
1990	385	22,904	1,188.60	51,895	$5,021	$219,219	$4.22
1995	370	26,995	1,262.80	46,779	$5,493	$203,482	$4.35
2000	461	35,597	1,420.00	39,891	$8,100	$227,547	$5.39
2003	459	35,361	1,574.00	44,512	$9,490	$268,375	$6.03

Admissions Per Screen is the total number of people per screen.

Scanning is looking for information quickly before or after you read a text. You can scan for numbers, symbols, bolded items, names, key words, or brief answers to questions. To scan:

1. Decide on what you want to find: a date, the name of a company, or the number of teens who use the Internet, for example.

2. Predict what you will be looking for: capital letters, numbers, or symbols, for instance.

3. Move your eyes quickly across the page—with the help of your finger or a pencil, if you want—looking only for the item you want to find.

Read the following question.

How many new pictures were released in 1985?

Refer to the table on the previous page. In order to find the answer, first scan the column *Year* and find *1985*. Then scan across the row to the *New Pictures Released* column to find the answer. You do not need to read the other columns or rows. The answer is *389*.

3 | Scanning

Scan the table for the answers to the questions. Discuss your answers with a partner.

1. In which year was the greatest number of new pictures released? _____

2. What were the total ticket sales per screen in 1980? _____

3. In which year was the average ticket price $4.35? _____

4. How many indoor screens were there in 1995? _____

5. Which year had the largest number of indoor screens? _____

4 | Discussing the Issues

Answer the questions and discuss your answers with a partner.

1. Do you think ticket prices affect whether people go to the movies? Why or why not?

2. Why might the data collected in the chart be important?

3. The table shows that while the total number of admissions has increased, the number of *admissions per screen* has, in general, decreased. What is a possible explanation for this?

Text 4 | Movies—Bollywood Style

1 | Getting Started

A. Answer the questions and briefly discuss your answers with a partner.

1. Check (✔) the movie genres that you enjoy.

☐ a. drama   ☐ d. action   ☐ g. comedy

☐ b. horror   ☐ e. musical   ☐ h. detective/crime mystery

☐ c. science fiction/fantasy   ☐ f. romance   ☐ i. western

2. Circle your favorite genre from the list in question *1*.

3. Check (✔) the features of your favorite movie genre.

☐ a. dramatic scenes   ☐ d. scary scenes   ☐ g. fantasy scenes

☐ b. action   ☐ e. singing and dancing   ☐ h. romance

☐ c. comedy   ☐ f. violence   ☐ i. adventure

4. What else should be in a good film? _____

B. Answer the questions and briefly discuss your answers with a partner.

1. Do you prefer Hollywood movies, movies made in your country, or movies made in other countries?

2. Why do you think some people might prefer movies made in their own countries?

3. What advantages may there be for a country that produces its own movies?

2 | Skipping Words and Phrases

A. Read the following sentences. First, cross out the words or phrases you do not understand. Then write their parts of speech on the blanks.

1. Bollywood churns out more than 800 films a year, which is even more than Hollywood produces. _____

2. He has now raised more than $500,000 from other techies and is executive producer of *My Bollywood Bride.* _____

3. At least another half dozen techies with Indian backgrounds have invested sums of up to $1 million in specific Bollywood films or studios. _____

4. Financing has improved due to more corporate filmmakers, proper insurance policies, and completion bonds. _____

5. Since the tax regime has changed, investors can expect sweeter returns from successful films. _____

B. With a partner, discuss what you do understand about each sentence.

3 | Active Previewing

REMEMBER
Preview longer academic texts a second time.

A. Preview the academic text below. Underline the title, the first sentence of each paragraph, and the last sentence of the text as you preview. Then tell a partner two things you remember about it.

B. Work as a class or in large groups. Try to name as many things as you can about the text.

C. Then answer this question with a partner.

What is this text about?

4 | Reading and Recalling

A. Read the text. Stop after each paragraph and tell a partner two things that you remember about it.

Bollywood Bonanza

by Nick Goodway

1 **Bollywood Background**

Imagine this movie: a sweeping desert landscape, evil villains, beautiful heroines, and mustachioed[1] heroes; plenty of loud music and exotic dancing; good always winning over evil—oh, and it must last at least three or four hours, so the audience feels they've had value for money. That is a quick definition of one of the world's fastest growing industries—Bollywood.

2 Bollywood, originally the name of a Mumbai suburb, is the name for the Indian film industry. It has grown at a rate of 25 percent a year for the past five years, according to the Federation of Indian Chambers of Commerce and Industry.

3 India's participation in the cinematic industry dates back 100 years. The first foreign film was shown in 1896, and the first Indian film appeared on the screens 17 years later. The

Devdas

film, *Rajah Harischandra*, was an extraordinary commercial success: Indians have been an enthusiastic movie-going public since the very beginning.

4 Bollywood churns out[2] more than 800 films a year, which is even more than Hollywood produces. Furthermore, it must be noted that Indian films are made in no fewer than 52 different languages with Hindi, Tamil, Telugu, Malayalam, and Kannada being the most common.

continued

---

[1] **mustachioed:** having a mustache, usually one that is large or long
[2] **to churn out:** to produce, to make

continued

5 **Investment Potential**

A good Bollywood movie costs between $1 million and $5 million to produce, whereas Hollywood considers $20 million to be low-budget. Now, from California to England, the industry is attracting the attention of those cash-rich, non-resident Indians (NRIs) as having excellent investment potential. There are an estimated 20 million NRIs with a combined net worth thought to be around $300 billion. In the United Kindom, for example, there are 2.5 million Asians, worth some $50 billion, who support 50 screens showing only Bollywood films and who watch the 23 Asian TV channels.

6 Following a heart attack, London resident Videk Wadhwa, the founder and former chief executive of Realtivity Technologies®, took a month-long break to visit his son back in India and caught the Bollywood bug. He has now raised more than $500,000 from other techies[3] and is executive producer of *My Bollywood Bride.*

7 At least another half dozen techies with Indian backgrounds have invested sums of up to $1 million in specific Bollywood films or studios. Now, there are even investment funds, such as the Isle of Man-based Bollywood Media and Entertainment Fund®, which aims to invest across the industry. Independent financial adviser Bobby Ailwadhi, who acts for the fund, says: "Bollywood is a core part of Asian culture, but the growing interest from the U.K. and other international markets has taken the Indian film industry to a different level."

8 The Indian entertainment industry's revenues are expected to double over the next few years. The growth comes not just from films but also from music, studios, magazines, videos and DVDs and, increasingly, satellite television. There is also a variety of support services including legal, banking, and distribution, which contribute to revenue.

9 A decade ago, a Bollywood hit would have made about 80 percent of its revenues from cinema distribution throughout India and the remainder from musical rights. Today the breakdown of revenues is more complex with nine percent from in-film advertising (mainly product placement), nine percent from satellite television rights, 29 percent from domestic theatres, 24 percent from music rights, and 29 percent from international distribution.

10 Indian producers tend to sell rights for a much shorter time scale of between three or five years, which gives them the chance to resell—possibly several times over. Financing has improved due to more corporate filmmakers, proper insurance policies, and completion bonds[4]. Rupert Murdoch's News Corp®, Universal®, and Sony® all have dedicated Indian film subsidiaries[5].

11 According to the Bollywood Media and Entertainment Fund®'s promoters, a Bollywood blockbuster earns five to ten times its costs, a super-hit three to five times costs, and a mere hit two to three times costs. Even a flop, or failure, they claim, usually recovers half its costs. Others are more cautious and prefer to point out that backers should only expect a one-in-ten chance of a blockbuster.

12 India had until recently the highest entertainment tax in the world, taking 50 percent of all cinema ticket revenues. However, since the tax regime has changed, investors can expect sweeter returns from successful films.

continued

[3] **techie:** (informal) a person who works or does research in a technical field
[4] **completion bond:** an agreement that requires one person or company to fulfill a contract or pay money to the other person or company if there is failure to do so
[5] **subsidiary:** a secondary company, or company that is dependent on a parent company

continued

13 The Public—In and Out of India

At the same time, things are moving quickly at the consumer end. Large-screen Imax® and various multiplex cinema chains have arrived. Furthermore, with a rapidly growing affluent middle class, cable and satellite television is growing as fast as movie theaters, if not more quickly, and providing second and third outlets for films.

14 However, despite the popularity of movies, India still remains underscreened. There are twelve screens per million people, compared to 75 screens per million people in Europe and 116 per million people in the U.S.

15 The speed at which the industry is changing is hard to measure. The world market has sat up and taken notice after the success of crossover films such as *Bend it Like Beckham* and *Monsoon Wedding.* But pure Indian productions such as *Laagan—Once Upon a Time in India, Kaante,* and *Devdas,* are attracting attention from non-Indians, as well.

16 Clearly, India is at a turning point in its cinematic ventures. Bollywood is featuring more western actors in its films, including more English in its dialogues, and producing films that center on the experiences of NRIs. The fact that the wholly Indian productions have caught the eye of international distributors including Columbia TriStar® shows that things are moving. On the one hand, Indian film is becoming increasingly westernized, and on the other, the West is increasingly interested in Indian cinema.

B. Read the text again without pausing. Tell your partner two new pieces of information that you remember.

C. Work as a class or in large groups. Try to name as many things as you can about the text.

5 | Understanding the Text

A. Answer as many questions as you can without looking at the text. Discuss your answers with a partner.

1. What is Bollywood?

a. the first Indian movie

b. the Indian film industry

c. an Indian technological firm

2. Generally speaking, how do Indians feel about movies?

    a. They have been enthusiastic about movies since the beginning.

    b. They have been interested in movies since the beginning of television.

    c. They are only recently interested in movies.

3. Who are some of the people who invest in Bollywood movies?

    a. Indian actors and actresses

    b. cash-rich non-resident Indians (NRIs)

    c. California computer firms

4. What is happening to the Indian entertainment industry?

    a. It is shrinking.

    b. It is staying about the same.

    c. It is growing.

5. What is one way in which Bollywood is at a turning point?

    a. Indian productions have caught the eye of international distributors.

    b. Despite the popularity of movies, India still remains underscreened.

    c. In the United Kingdom, there are 2.5 million Asians who watch 23 Asian TV channels.

6. How much does a Bollywood blockbuster earn?

    a. two to three times its costs

    b. three to five times its costs

    c. five to ten times its costs

B. Check (✔) the correct answers according to the text. Discuss your answers with a partner.

Event	Bollywood	Hollywood
1. This industry has grown at a rate of 25% a year for the past five years.	☐	☐
2. This place makes fewer movies.	☐	☐
3. This place considers $20 million a low budget for making a movie.	☐	☐
4. Here, the flops, or failures, earn half their costs, they claim.	☐	☐
5. It is difficult to measure how fast this industry is changing.	☐	☐

6 | Discussing the Issues

Answer the questions and discuss your answers with a partner.

1. Would you invest money in a Bollywood movie? Why or why not?

2. Why do you think that a foreign movie industry, such as Bollywood, might want to incorporate western actors into its movies?

3. Do you think that people in your country should see movies from other countries? Why or why not?

Putting It On Paper

A. Write a paragraph on one of these topics.

1. Are movies a good form of entertainment? Describe why they are or are not.

2. Are foreign movies a good way to learn about a different country or culture? Describe why they are or are not.

Steps for your paragraph

    a. State your opinion in the first sentence; this is your thesis statement or topic sentence.

    b. Give three details—for example, facts, data, examples—that prove or illustrate your opinion.

    c. Summarize your ideas in a final sentence.

B. Exchange paragraphs with a partner. First, read your partner's paragraph and answer the questions in the checklist. Then give feedback to your partner.

✔ CHECKLIST
1. Can you identify your partner's opinion about the topic?
2. Are there three examples to support the topic? Number them.
3. Do your partner's examples or reasons persuade you? Explain.
4. Is any of the information not related to the topic? If yes, please underline it on your partner's paper, and then write it here:

_____

_____

_____

_____

_____

_____

C. Revise your work based on your partner's feedback.

Taking It Online | "Action!"

A. With a partner, use the Internet to research movies and movie-makers.

1. Use Google (www.google.com) or another major search engine to begin your online research.

2. Search for websites with information about one actor, one director, and one movie.

3. Preview the websites.

ONLINE TIP

Use quotation marks in the search box to search for word groups or phrases:
"gong li"
"pedro almodovar"
"african queen"

B. Complete the tables with the information you find.

Actor
Name:
Website address:
Fact 1:
Fact 2:

Director
Name:
Website address:
Fact 1:
Fact 2:

Movie
Name:
Website address:
Fact 1:
Fact 2:

C. Following up. Tell your classmates the facts you discovered. See if they can guess which actor, director, and movie you researched.

Chapter 2

The Science of Love

Answer the questions and briefly discuss your answers with a partner.

1. Are you in, or do you know someone in, a long-term relationship?

2. What are some common ways people meet?

3. What kinds of relationships are shown in the photos?

Text 1 | Online Dating

1 | Getting Started

A. Answer the questions and briefly discuss your answers with a partner.

1. Have you heard of Internet dating?

2. Do you know anyone who has used the Internet to meet other people? If so, who? If you can, describe that person's experience.

3. Why do you think some people use the Internet to meet other people?

B. Complete the chart with three possible advantages and three possible disadvantages of meeting someone online. Briefly discuss your answers with a partner.

Advantages	Disadvantages
1.	1.
2.	2.
3.	3.

2 | Active Previewing

A. Preview the online article on the next page and tell a partner two things you remember about it.

B. Work as a class or in large groups. Try to name as many things as you can about the text.

C. Then answer this question with a partner.

What is this text about?

> **REMEMBER**
>
> Preview online articles by reading the title, the first sentence of each paragraph, and the final sentence of the text. For more on *previewing online articles*, see page 3.

3 | Reading and Recalling

A. Read the text. Stop after each paragraph and tell a partner two things that you remember about it.

Online Dating Do's and Don'ts

by Pepper Schwartz, Ph.D.

1   Considering online dating, but feeling nervous? Believe me, you're not the only one. Putting yourself out there takes guts, or courage. But the Internet is a great way to meet fun, eligible[1] people. Here are my tips for staying safe and having a good time:

REMEMBER
Skip the words and phrases you do not understand. For more about *skipping words*, see page 2.

2   DO get specific in your online profile. Write about yourself in a way that paints a vivid (clear) picture of who you are. Don't just say you love to travel; include a vignette—a brief story—about your journey to Africa. Or talk about the political issues that really get you riled up[2]. Write the way you speak, not the way you would write an essay! How is someone going to be interested if you just say you love dogs and movies?

3   DON'T disclose too much personal information. No matter how charming your online pen pal is, no one deserves your telephone number until you've found out lots of background information about him or her. Always arrange to meet for coffee *before* giving an online prospect, or possible date, your contact information. That way, the person won't be able to keep calling after you've decided you're not interested. And never give out a home address until after you've gone on a few dates!

4   DO spend time getting to know someone. One of the wonderful things about beginning a relationship online is the opportunity to develop real intimacy, or closeness. Exchanging e-mail is a great way to get to know someone. Even if you choose a potential online date because of his or her photo, make sure to spend some time writing each other about your hobbies, opinions and beliefs, family, and dreams. The longer you chat before actually meeting, the better it will be when you finally meet! Cultivating, or encouraging, a real dialogue may also give your relationship a solid start.

5   DO give someone the chance to impress you. When communicating with someone for the first time, you may think this person isn't enough like you or isn't attractive and quickly decide not to meet. But you could be depriving[3] yourself of a fantastic opportunity if you don't give this person a second chance. Don't be rigid (inflexible); first impressions aren't always the whole story. Give yourself—and your online date—time to warm up to each other before deciding to give up.

6   DON'T tell little white lies. Be honest online because it's the right thing to do—and

continued

---

[1] **eligible:** qualified to be chosen; here, available for marriage, or single
[2] **riled (up):** angry
[3] **to deprive:** to prevent from enjoying

continued

because you will have to live with the consequences of any fibs you tell. Many people have told me how angry they were when they met their online date for a drink and found that the person was 30 pounds heavier or 20 years older than he or she claimed to be. Don't exaggerate, or overstate, your credentials or use the photo that makes you look like a professional model. Don't set yourself up to be a disappointment. You want to *exceed* expectations.

7   DON'T do all the talking. It's so much fun to express yourself online that you might not realize your potential date has not been typing much back. Or you might feel so nervous when you talk on the phone that you monopolize—dominate—the conversation. It's important that you give the other person time to talk and that you listen attentively[4]. You need to know as much as possible about the other person so you'll be able to decide if you should meet in the real world.

8   DO be happy. A good attitude is important. I don't care if someone kidnapped your dog or fired you on your birthday. If you are even a little bit depressed or angry, you can kiss your chances of developing a serious connection goodbye. Topics to avoid: old relationships, an unfulfilled yearning (desire) for children, and a deep mistrust of others. It's not that people with troubles can't find love, but until another person gets to know all your positive traits, or characteristics, he or she won't realize that you aren't angry at the world. Be optimistic[5] that you will find an amazing person. You probably will!

---

[4] **attentive:** giving care or attention
[5] **optimistic:** expecting a good outcome

B. Read the text again without pausing. Tell your partner two new pieces of information that you remember.

C. Work as a class or in large groups. Try to name as many things as you can about the text.

4 | Understanding the Text

A. Complete the chart without looking at the text. Discuss your answers with a partner.

Online Dating Do's	Online Dating Don'ts
1. get specific in your profile	1.
2.	2.
3.	3.
4.	4.

B. Write *T* for *True* and *F* for *False* according to the text. Discuss your answers with a partner.

___F___ 1. Write your profile the same way you would write an essay.

_____ 2. Always arrange to meet for coffee before giving your contact information.

_____ 3. If you aren't impressed with someone the first time you communicate, give the person a second chance.

_____ 4. Don't worry about being honest online.

_____ 5. It is important that you talk more than the other person to get over your nervousness but also that you listen attentively.

READING SKILL Understanding the Topic

The **topic** is the subject of a text or a paragraph. The topic is always expressed as a word or a phrase (not a complete sentence). To identify the topic:

1. Choose a word or phrase that most closely describes the subject of the whole paragraph or text.

2. Do not choose a topic that is too general.

3. Do not choose a topic that is too specific.

Reread ¶2 on page 23. The possible choices for the topic are:

    a. a profile

    b. including a vignette in your profile

    c. writing an online profile

Choice *a* is too general. It does not say what kind of profile is discussed in ¶2, and it does not say what aspect of a profile is important.

Choice *b* is too specific. It is only one detail in the paragraph.

Choice *c* is the best topic for ¶2.

5 | Understanding the Topic

A. Text. Write *T* for *Topic*, *G* for *Too General*, and *S* for *Too Specific*. Discuss your answers with a partner.

1. What is the topic of the text?

    a. _____ dating and relationships

    b. _____ creating an online profile for an Internet date

    c. _____ Internet dating

2. Is your answer for the topic of the text the same as the one you determined after you previewed the text, or is your answer different? _____

B. Paragraphs. Write *T* for *Topic*, *G* for *Too General*, and *S* for *Too Specific*. Discuss your answers with a partner.

1. What is the topic for ¶3?

    a. _____ meeting an online date for coffee

    b. _____ disclosing personal information to an online date

    c. _____ background information

2. What is the topic for ¶4?

    a. _____ getting to know someone

    b. _____ choosing an online date by his or her photo

    c. _____ getting to know someone online

3. What is the topic for ¶5?

    a. _____ first impressions

    b. _____ giving an online date a second chance

    c. _____ what to do if an online date isn't attractive

Vocab **VOCABULARY STRATEGY** Understanding Vocabulary in Context— Synonyms

One strategy for understanding unfamiliar words is to look for **synonyms**. Synonyms are words that have the same or a similar meaning. Synonyms of potentially unfamiliar words are often set apart from the main sentence by commas (,), dashes (—), or parentheses (( )).

Read the following sentences.

1. Putting yourself out there takes guts, or courage. (¶1)

    What are *guts*? The comma (,) + *or* indicate that *guts* means *courage*.

2. Don't just say you love to travel; include a vignette—a brief story—about your journey to Africa. (¶2)

    What is a *vignette*? The dashes (—) that surround *a brief story* indicate that *vignette* means *a brief story*.

3. Don't be rigid (inflexible); first impressions aren't always the whole story. (¶5)

    What does *rigid* mean? The parentheses (( )) indicate that *rigid* means *inflexible*.

6 | Understanding Vocabulary in Context—Synonyms

Write the best synonym for each word according to the text. Discuss your answers with a partner.

1. prospect (¶3) _possible date_

2. to cultivate (¶4) _____

3. to exaggerate (¶6) _____

4. to monopolize (¶7) _____

5. yearning (¶8) _____

7 | Discussing the Issues

Answer the questions and discuss your answers with a partner.

1. What do you think of Dr. Schwartz's advice? Choose two pieces of her advice that you think are valuable or two pieces of advice that you do not think are valuable, and explain why.

2. Do you think the Internet is or could be a good place to meet people? Would you ever recommend online dating to a friend?

3. Imagine that a friend of yours is thinking about joining on online dating service. Think about Dr. Schwartz's advice. What would you tell your friend?

Text 2 | Love at First Smell

1 | Getting Started

A. Answer the questions and briefly discuss your answers with a partner.

1. Check (✔) the qualities that are important in a friend or romantic partner.

A friend or romantic partner should be:		
☐ a. strong	☐ d. healthy	☐ g. reliable
☐ b. nice smelling	☐ e. financially stable	☐ h. physically attractive
☐ c. intelligent	☐ f. trustworthy	☐ i. polite

2. Why are the qualities that you checked important?

B. Check (✔) the statements that are true. Briefly discuss your answers with a partner.

☐ **1.** Every person is born with a particular smell type.

☐ **2.** Some smells can bring back memories or change our mood.

☐ **3.** A person's natural smell is inherited from his or her parents.

☐ **4.** The sense of smell is one of our most important senses.

☐ **5.** Perfume covers up a person's natural smell.

READING SKILL Previewing Newspaper Articles

Newspaper articles usually order information from the most important to the least important. To **preview** a newspaper article:

1. Read the title.

2. Look at any photos, and read the captions.

3. Read the first two to four paragraphs.

Paragraphs two to four usually answer the questions *Who? What? When? Where?* The rest of the article gives the details.

---

2 | Active Previewing

A. Preview the newspaper article on the next page by reading the first two paragraphs. Then answer the questions and discuss your answers with a partner.

1. **Who** has done the research?

2. **Where** does he do the research?

3. **What** does the research show?

4. **When** do people react to the odor that everyone is born with?

B. Work as a class or in large groups. Try to name as many things as you can about the text.

C. Then answer this question with a partner.

What is the topic of this newspaper article?

3 | Reading and Recalling

A. Read the text. Stop after each subtitled section and tell a partner two things that you remember about it.

Smelling Out the Perfect Soul-Mate

BY PAUL CAREY

1 A Question of Smell

We may all think that people choose their perfect partners based on their appearance, personality, or even the size of their wallet, but research on how we choose a mate by a Welsh expert reveals the key to finding a soul-mate is the way he or she smells.

2 Professor Tim Jacob is head of the smell research laboratory in the School of Biosciences at Cardiff University. He claims that when finding the perfect partner, people are reacting to the subtle, or slight, odor that everyone is born with.

3 Prof. Jacob claims this phenomenon[1] is nature's way of ensuring, or guaranteeing, that children are born with the strongest immune systems possible to fight off disease.

4 Opposites Attract

And when it comes to finding a husband or wife, the research reveals that opposites do attract.

5 "This is a subtle smell—it's not the sweaty body odor someone has after doing hard manual labor for a few days without washing," Jacob said. "This is an inherent[2] smell that we all carry; you can't change it by washing or perfume."

6 In a review commissioned by the medicine manufacturer Sudafed®, Prof. Jacob has found that every person is born with a certain odor-type, which is dependent on his or her immuno-type, or immunogenetic status. This immuno-type is the body's own defense mechanism, or protection, against disease and illness.

7 Prof. Jacob said there are thousands of different immuno- and odor-types, but rather than seek out people with a similar smell, humans prefer to bond[3] with people who have a different odor-type. This is to ensure that any children born as a result of their union will inherit two different immuno-types, thus bolstering their natural defense systems against disease.

8 Research has shown that women prefer male odors that are different from their own genetic makeup; the smell from men with the same genetic make-up is found to be unpleasant.

9 Marriages between people with similar genetic make-up are not as frequent as expected, and a high degree of genetic similarity between parents could even increase the chances of miscarriage.

10 "Diversity is key—nature is trying to bring together two people who will provide immuno-diversity to their offspring; therefore, the child will have the benefit of both parents and increased disease resistance," Jacob said.

11 How We Use Smell

Prof. Jacob added, "Smell is the most underrated of the major senses. It's one of the most important senses we have, but most people do not understand the true significance of smell."

> **REMEMBER**
> Skip the words and phrases you do not understand.

12 Odor-types are not the same as pheromones[4], which some believe play an important role in social and chemical interaction.

13 Sniffer dogs use odor-types to distinguish individuals. The research reveals that not only do humans, too, use smell to distinguish between individuals, but also that they actively select their mates based on odor-type.

14 Unlike any of the other senses, smell has direct access to the more primitive, or basic, parts of the brain. Brain imaging techniques have shown that smell can activate mood, emotion, and memory without being consciously perceived.

15 The main source of human odor is the apocrine glands, or sweat glands. They are found in various parts of the body, including underarms, hair follicles, cheeks, eyelids, ears, and scalp.

16 When they kiss, people are also "tasting" the other person's odor-type, which in turn will help determine whether that person is the perfect mate.

continued

---

[1] **phenomenon:** an occurrence or fact that can be perceived by the senses

[2] **inherent:** existing as an essential part of

[3] **to bond:** to grow close to

[4] **pheromones:** substances produced by animals that produce a response from other members of that species

continued

17 Perfume and Odor-Types

Smell can trigger[5] memories, evoke disgust, pleasure, or change our mood. It can act as a warning or can be a sign of illness. So the sensory shutdown associated with a cold or flu infection can have more far-reaching consequences than had ever previously been considered.

18   Even the type of perfume a person wears says more about him or her than previously thought. Rather than using perfumes to smell sweet, it is now believed that we choose them on the basis of how close they are to our own immuno-type.

19   If a group of people is offered a selection of different perfume ingredients, such as woody or floral tones, those with the same immuno-types will prefer the same type of perfume ingredients, according to Prof. Jacob.

20   "What we are doing in choosing a certain perfume ingredient is advertising our immuno-types to others, our potential partners," Jacob added.

21   "We are now beginning to understand the mechanisms by which smell can influence our first impressions of potential partners."

---

[5] **to trigger:** to cause, to set off

B. Read the text again without pausing. Tell your partner two new pieces of information that you remember.

C. Work as a class or in large groups. Try to name as many things as you can about the text.

4 | Understanding the Text

A. Answer the questions without looking at the text. Discuss your answers with a partner.

1. What is one of the major factors involved in how we choose a mate?

2. Do people typically choose mates whose odors are the same or different from their own?

3. What influences people's choice of perfume?

B. Check (✔) the three statements that are mentioned in the text. Discuss your answers with a partner.

☐ **1.** When it comes to finding a husband or wife, opposites do attract.

☐ **2.** Humans prefer to bond with people who have a different odor type.

☐ **3.** According to research, smell helps us hear well.

☐ **4.** A person's immuno-type is the body's own defense mechanism against disease.

5 | Understanding the Topic

Text. Write *T* for *Topic*, *G* for *Too General*, and *S for Too Specific*. Discuss your answers with a partner.

1. What is the topic of the text?

a. _____ people's choice of perfumes

b. _____ the role of smell in choosing a mate

c. _____ the sense of smell

2. Is your answer for the topic the same as the one you determined after you previewed the text, or is your answer different? _____

VOCABULARY STRATEGY Understanding Subject and Object Pronouns

Pronouns refer to nouns. We use pronouns to avoid repeating the same nouns over and over again. Usually, a pronoun refers to the closest and/or most logical noun (or pronoun) that comes before it in a sentence or paragraph.

A **subject pronoun** replaces a noun used as the subject of a sentence or clause. The subject pronouns are: **I, you, he, she, it, we, you,** and **they.**

Read the following examples.

1. Research by a Welsh expert on how we choose a mate reveals the key to finding a soul-mate is the way *he* or *she* smells. (¶1)

   Soul-mate is the closest and the most logical noun that comes before *he* or *she* in the paragraph. Therefore, *he* or *she* refers to *soul-mate.*

   Note: When a pronoun is in a dependant clause, it often refers to the noun that appears after it.

2. When *they* kiss, people are also "tasting" the other person's odor-type. (¶16)

   The pronoun *they* is in a dependant clause in this sentence; *they* refers to *people* which appears after the pronoun.

   _____

An **object pronoun** replaces a noun used as the object of a sentence, clause, or phrase. The object pronouns are **me, you, him, her, it, us, you,** and **them.**

Read the following examples.

1. This is an inherent smell that we all carry—you can't change *it* by washing or perfume. (¶5)

   Smell is not the nearest noun or pronoun, but it is the most logical. Therefore, it refers to smell.

   Note: Sometimes *we* does not refer to a noun in the text. Rather, *we* is used in a general sense to indicate "we the readers" or sometimes "we human beings."

2. *We* may all think that people choose their perfect partners based on their appearance, personality, or even the size of their wallet. (¶1)

   Note: Sometimes *it* does not refer to a noun in the text, but is used as the subject of a sentence stating a general truth or fact: *It's really hot out today* or *It's such a beautiful day.*

3. And when *it* comes to finding a husband or wife, the research reveals that opposites do attract. (¶4)

6 | Understanding Subject and Object Pronouns

Write the subject or object that the pronoun refers to according to the text. Discuss your answers with a partner.

1. He (He claims) (¶2) _____

2. it (it's one of the most) (¶11) _____

3. they (they actively select) (¶13) _____

4. They (They are found) (¶15) _____

5. they (when they kiss) (¶16) _____

6. It (It can act) (¶17) _____

7. him or her (more about him or her) (¶18) _____

8. them (choose them) (¶18) _____

7 | Understanding Vocabulary in Context—Synonyms

Write the best synonym for each word or phrase according to the text. Discuss your answers with a partner.

1. subtle (¶2) _slight_____

2. to ensure (¶3) _____

3. defense mechanism (¶6) _____

4. primitive (¶14) _____

5. apocrine glands (¶15) _____

8 | Discussing the Issues

Answer the questions and discuss your answers with a partner.

1. According to the text, smell plays a part in how people choose their mates. After having read the text, do you find this idea to be reasonable? Why or why not?

2. How might a cold or flu affect a person's ability to choose a mate?

3. Do you think that smell could also play a role in how people choose their friends? Why or why not?

Text 3 | The Best First Date

1 | Getting Started

Answer the questions and briefly discuss your answers with a partner.

1. What is your gender?

   ☐ male　　☐ female

2. What is the best plan for a first date? Check (✔) only one box.

   ☐ a. going to lunch or dinner

   ☐ b. meeting for coffee

   ☐ c. going to a movie

   ☐ d. going to an event (e.g., concert or play)

   ☐ e. going to the beach or a park

3. Do you think men and women agree about what makes a good first date? Why or why not?

GRAPHICS Previewing Graphs and Charts

Graphs and charts give a picture of statistical information. **Pie charts** are one type of chart that shows statistical information in the shape of a pie. Each "slice of pie" represents a part of the whole. A larger slice represents a larger percentage than the smaller slices. **Preview** graphs and charts by reading the title and any subtitles or category headings.

---

2 | Active Previewing

Preview the pie charts on the next page, and then answer the questions. Discuss your answers with a partner.

1. What is the title of the pie chart survey?

2. What are the titles of the two pie charts?

3. What is the topic of these pie charts?

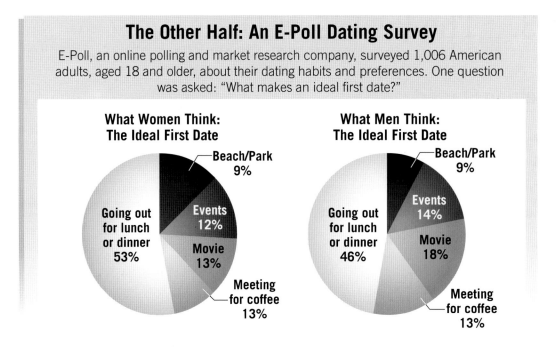

The Other Half: An E-Poll Dating Survey

E-Poll, an online polling and market research company, surveyed 1,006 American adults, aged 18 and older, about their dating habits and preferences. One question was asked: "What makes an ideal first date?"

What Women Think: The Ideal First Date

Beach/Park 9%
Events 12%
Movie 13%
Meeting for coffee 13%
Going out for lunch or dinner 53%

What Men Think: The Ideal First Date

Beach/Park 9%
Events 14%
Movie 18%
Meeting for coffee 13%
Going out for lunch or dinner 46%

3 | Scanning

Scan the pie charts for the answers to the questions. Discuss your answers with a partner.

1. How many adults did E-Poll survey? __1,006__

2. What percentage of women think that meeting for coffee is an ideal first date? _____

3. What is the most popular ideal first date for men? _____

4. Who prefers going to a movie for an ideal first date more, men or women? _____

5. What is the least popular first date for women? _____

4 | Discussing the Issues

Answer the questions and discuss your answers with a partner.

1. If E-Poll conducted this survey with your friends, would the results be the same or different? Why?

2. E-Poll divided their results into Women and Men. What do you think the results might have looked like if they had divided their results by age groups (i.e., 18-30, 31-49, 50+)?

3. Work with a partner to collect your classmates' answers to *Getting Started*, questions *1* and *2*, on the previous page. How closely do your class results match the results of the E-Poll survey?

Text 4 | Close Friends

1 | Getting Started

A. Answer the questions and briefly discuss your answers with a partner.

1. Do you live near any of your friends?

2. Do you think it is important to live near your friends?

3. Do you think people are more likely to become friends with someone who lives nearby? Why or why not?

B. Complete the chart about how you met three of your friends. Briefly discuss your answers with a partner.

| Friend's name | I first saw this person... | | We became friends... | |
	When?	Where?	How long after?	How?
Maria	on the first day of science class	in high school	one month later	We were partners on a science project.
1.				
2.				
3.				

2 | Active Previewing

A. Preview the academic text on the next page and tell a partner two things you remember about it.

B. Work as a class or in large groups. Try to name as many things as you can about the text.

C. Then answer this question with a partner.

What is the topic of this text?

REMEMBER

Preview the text by reading the title, the subtitles, the first sentence of each paragraph, and the final sentence of the text. Preview longer academic texts a second time. For more about *previewing academic texts*, see page 3.

A. Read the text. Stop after each paragraph and tell a partner two things that you remember about it.

Meeting Strangers: Proximity and Emotions

by Robert A. Baron and Donn Byrne

1 Though there are about six billion people on this planet, we are likely to interact with only a very small percentage of them. Among these people, some become acquaintances and some remain strangers. Why? Our physical surroundings strongly influence whom we are likely to meet. Simply stated, two people will probably become acquainted if they are brought into regular contact through physical proximity (closeness) and if each of them is experiencing positive rather than negative affect (feelings or mood) at the time.

2 **Physical Surroundings: Repeated Interpersonal Contact Leads to Attraction**

Casual and unplanned contacts soon lead to mutual, or shared, recognition. When two strangers regularly pass one another in the hallway, sit next to each other in class, or wait together every morning at the bus stop, they begin to become familiar to each other. Next, they may begin exchanging a brief greeting when they meet ("Hi") and maybe a word or two about the weather or some newsworthy[1] event. In other words, a familiar face evokes[2] positive feelings. Even infants tend to smile at a photograph of someone they have seen before, but not at a photograph of someone they are seeing for the first time (Brooks-Gunn & Lewis, 1981).

3 **Why Does Repeated Contact Increase Interpersonal Attraction?**

Zajonc (1968) proposed that repeated exposure to, or frequent contact with, a person leads to a more and more positive evaluation of him or her. The general idea is that we often feel at least slightly uncomfortable with anyone new. With repeated exposure, the feelings of anxiety (nervousness) decrease, and the new someone gradually becomes familiar. That is, people begin to feel friendly toward strangers sitting right next to them in class because they see those individuals over and over again. In the same class, students who sit in different rows are harder to see, so familiarity and friendship don't develop.

4 To show just how this process operates, Moreland and Beach (1992) asked one female research assistant to attend a college class fifteen times during the semester, a second research assistant to attend ten times, a third to attend five times, and a fourth research assistant not to attend at all. Then, at the end of the semester, all four of them came to the classroom, and the researchers asked all students in the class to rate how much they liked each of the four women. The assistants were fairly similar in appearance, and none interacted with any of the students during the semester. Nevertheless, attraction increased as the number of classroom exposures increased.

> **REMEMBER**
> Skip the words and phrases you do not understand.
> For more about *skipping words,* see page 2.

5 It is important to understand that the repeated exposure effect does not apply to a new person if the initial (first) reaction is very negative. Research confirms the fact that repeated exposure to someone who evokes quite negative feelings does not result in increased liking (Swap, 1977). Additional contact with a disliked person can actually maximize, or increase, the initial feeling of dislike. In most interpersonal situations the initial reaction to a stranger tends to be neutral[3]

continued

---

[1] **newsworthy:** interesting or remarkable
[2] **to evoke:** to suggest, bring to mind
[3] **neutral:** impartial; not taking sides

continued

or mildly positive, so what are the effects of repeated exposure to others in real-life settings?

6 Residential Proximity: Friendship and Marriage

Studies over the past few decades are consistent in finding that as the distance between residences (people's homes) decreases, random contact between the residents becomes more frequent, and positive relationships develop between them. For example, studies of multistoried[4] undergraduate dormitories showed that two-thirds of friendships develop among people living on the same floor, and only rarely do students get to know those living more than one floor away (Evans & Wilson, 1949; Lundberg & Beazley, 1948). Almost fifty years after those studies were conducted, Whitbeck and Hoyt (1994) found that the choice of dating partners among undergraduates is in part related to the distance between the partners' college residences.

7   Proximity not only results in people's becoming acquainted, it even influences dating and marriage. Two of the oldest studies showing a relationship between the physical environment and attraction were conducted in the 1930s. In Philadelphia, Bossard (1932) examined the first 5,000 marriages performed in 1931 and then determined where the bride and groom lived before the wedding. About a third of the couples lived within five blocks of one another before they married, and more than half lived within a twenty-block radius. A few years later, the study was repeated in New Haven with the records of 1,000 marriages in 1931, and almost identical results were obtained (Davie & Reeves, 1939). The closer the residences of a man and a woman, the greater the probability they will marry.

8   The investigators in the studies above demonstrated a clear connection between distance and attraction. However, they could not conclude with certainty that the subjects' relationships developed simply because of their close proximity to each other. Perhaps people who share other characteristics (such as religion, race, social class, etc.) prefer to live near one another. If so, these other factors may have influenced proximity and attraction, rather than proximity influencing attraction.

9 Manipulating Proximity to Determine Its Effects

Obviously, it is not possible or reasonable for an experimenter to manipulate, or control, where people live or work in order to study interpersonal attraction. On the other hand, such manipulation often does occur in the college setting. When administrators or instructors make random assignments of housing or seating, for example, they create the necessary conditions for an experiment.

10   Couples assigned to random apartments in married student housing become acquainted on the basis of proximity. This has provided strong evidence that proximity leads to a better chance of becoming acquainted. For example, couples whose apartments are located within 22 feet of one another are quite likely to become acquainted; in contrast, such relationships are quite *un*likely if the apartments are more than 88 feet apart (Festinger, Schachter, & Back, 1950).

11   In a similar way, at the beginning of a semester, students are randomly assigned to classroom seats, and relationships develop during the semester according to the distance between seats. This, too, indicates[5] that proximity influences which students become acquainted. For example, students assigned to a middle seat in a row are much more likely to become acquainted with the two students sitting closest to them (those sitting to their right and left) than to get to know any other students in the class (Byrne & Beuhler, 1955). When a student is assigned to the end of a row, fewer relationships develop than if the seat is elsewhere in the row (Maisonneuve, Palmade, & Fourment, 1952). If random seat assignments are made alphabetically, friendships form between those whose last names begin with the same or a

continued

---

[4] **multistoried:** having several floors
[5] **to indicate:** to point out, show

continued

nearby letter (Segal, 1974). Finally, if the instructor makes new seat assignments at various times during the semester, more students will become acquainted than if they must remain in one location all semester (Byrne, 1961).

12   Students who are free to choose their own classroom seats may want to apply what they have learned about proximity effects. For example, if a student wants to make new friends, he or she should obviously avoid the seats on the ends of rows; and if it is possible to change seats from day to day, the student should do so and increase the number of potential new acquaintances. If he or she *doesn't* want new friends for reasons of privacy (Larson & Bell, 1988), the student should select a seat in the back of the room, as far from others as possible (Pedersen, 1994).

B. Read the text again without pausing. Tell your partner two new pieces of information that you remember.

C. Work as a class or in large groups. Try to name as many things as you can about the text.

4 | Understanding the Text

A. Answer the questions without looking at the text. Discuss your answers with a partner.

1. Under what conditions are people most likely to meet and become acquainted?

2. How does repeated exposure affect initial feelings of anxiety?

3. Which research assistant did the students prefer in the university study?

4. How can proximity influence dating and marriage?

5. Why might students assigned to a seat at the end of a row develop fewer relationships than if he or she sat elsewhere in the row?

B. Check (✔) what is more likely without looking at the text. Discuss your answers with a partner.

More likely because of proximity and repeated exposure...	
☐ 1. forming friendships	☐ 5. choosing a university
☐ 2. choosing a pet	☐ 6. buying a house from someone
☐ 3. choosing a dating partner	☐ 7. eating at a certain restaurant
☐ 4. becoming friends with someone whom one did not like at first	☐ 8. choosing a husband or wife

5 | Understanding the Topic

A. Text. Write *T* for *Topic,* *G* for *Too General,* and *S* for *Too Specific.* Discuss your answers with a partner.

1. What is the topic of the text?

    a. _____ the effect of proximity on marriage

    b. _____ the nature of relationships

    c. _____ the effect of proximity on relationships

2. Is your answer for the topic the same as the one you determined after you previewed the text, or is your answer different? _____

B. Paragraphs. Write *T* for *Topic,* *G* for *Too General,* and *S* for *Too Specific.* Discuss your answers with a partner.

1. What is the topic of ¶3?

    a. _____ repeated exposure

    b. _____ effects of repeated exposure to a person

    c. _____ decreasing feelings of anxiety because of exposure to a person

2. What is the topic of ¶4?

    a. _____ the attraction for the research assistant who attended class the most

    b. _____ female research assistants

    c. _____ a familiarity experiment that used four female research assistants in a class

3. What is the topic of ¶7?

    a. _____ how proximity influences dating and marriage

    b. _____ dating and marriage

    c. _____ 5,000 marriages performed in 1931

4. What is the topic of ¶10?

    a. _____ how proximity affects relationships among couples in married student housing

    b. _____ relationships among married students who live 22 feet apart

    c. _____ married student housing

5. What is the topic of ¶11?

    a. _____ how classroom seating arrangements affect student relationships

    b. _____ how students sitting in the middle of a classroom form relationships

    c. _____ relationships between students in a classroom

6 | Understanding Subject and Object Pronouns

1. What subject or object do the pronouns from ¶1 refer to?

   a. we (we are likely) _we the readers OR we human beings_

   b. them (a very small percentage of them) _____

   c. we (we are likely to meet) _____

   d. they (they are brought into regular contact) _____

   e. them (if each of them) _____

2. What subject or object do the pronouns from ¶3 refer to?

   a. him or her (evaluation of him or her) _____

   b. we (we often feel) _____

   c. them (sitting right next to them) _____

3. What subject or object do the pronouns from ¶12 refer to?

   a. they (they have learned) _____

   b. he or she (he or she should obviously avoid) _____

   c. he or she (he or she *doesn't* want) _____

7 | Understanding Vocabulary in Context—Synonyms

Write the best synonym for each word according to the text. Discuss your answers with a partner.

1. physical proximity (¶1) _closeness_ _____

2. affect (¶1) _____

3. mutual (¶2) _____

4. repeated exposure to (¶3) _____

5. anxiety (¶3) _____

6. initial (¶5) _____

7. to maximize (¶5) _____

8. to manipulate (¶9) _____

8 | Discussing the Issues

Answer the questions and discuss your answers with a partner.

1. Do you agree with the research that says that frequent exposure to a new person leads to more positive feelings about that person? Why or why not?

2. Think about the people you have met in class. How has your opinion about these people changed over time?

3. How does your behavior at school influence your relationships with your classmates?

Putting It On Paper

A. Write a three-paragraph letter on one of these topics.

1. A friend of yours has moved to a new town to attend a new school or university or for a new job. Your friend doesn't know anyone in this town. Offer him or her advice, and compare and contrast the advantages/disadvantages of your suggestions.

2. A friend of yours is thinking about trying to meet someone through an Internet dating service. What kind of advice can you give your friend? Compare and contrast the advantages/disadvantages of your suggestions.

Steps for your letter

a. In your first paragraph, clearly show that you understand your friend's situation or wish.

b. In your second paragraph, offer three suggestions to your friend. You should also compare and contrast each suggestion in terms of how likely it is to help your friend succeed.

c. In your final paragraph, state which suggestion you think is best and perhaps show some concern or wishes for good luck—make the letter sound natural.

B. Exchange letters with a partner. First, read your partner's letter and answer the questions in the checklist. Then give feedback to your partner.

✓ CHECKLIST
1. Does ¶1 clearly show what new situation the friend is in or desire he or she has?
2. Does ¶2 offer three suggestions and discuss the advantages and disadvantages of each suggestion?
3. Does ¶3 state the preferred suggestion?
4. Are you persuaded by your partner's suggestion(s)?
5. Is there any information in the essay that is not related to your partner's suggestions? If yes, please underline it on your partner's paper, and write it here:

_____

_____

_____

_____

_____

_____

_____

C. Revise your letter based on your partner's feedback.

Taking It Online | Dating Customs

A. With a partner, use the Internet to research dating customs and traditions in different countries and cultures.

ONLINE TIP

Use CTRL+F to help you search a website for key words.

1. Use Google (www.google.com) or another major search engine to begin your online research.

2. Search for websites with information about dating customs in three different countries—one website for each country. (Consider typing "dating customs" and the country name in the search field.)

3. Preview the websites.

B. Complete the table with the information you find.

Country 1		
Name:		
Website address:		
Is dating common before marriage? ☐ yes ☐ no	At what age—if at all—do boys and girls begin dating?	Who is expected to pay for a date?
Country 2		
Name:		
Website address:		
Is dating common before marriage? ☐ yes ☐ no	At what age—if at all—do boys and girls begin dating?	Who is expected to pay for a date?
Country 3		
Name:		
Website address:		
Is dating common before marriage? ☐ yes ☐ no	At what age—if at all—do boys and girls begin dating?	Who is expected to pay for a date?

C. Following up. In small groups, discuss how you think dating customs in the countries you researched are similar and/or different to the dating customs in your country or culture.

Unnatural Resources

Answer the questions and briefly discuss your answers with a partner.

1. Do people ever throw away anything valuable?

2. Look at the photos. Which of the objects, if any, are valuable?

3. What is the original purpose of each object? In what other ways can these objects be used?

Text 1 | Trash or Treasure

1 | Getting Started

A. Answer the questions and briefly discuss your answers with a partner.

1. What are five items you have recently thrown away?

2. What are three things that can happen to trash after we throw it away?

3. Check (✔) all the words that are synonyms for *garbage* and *to throw away*.

garbage			to throw away		
☐ a. junk	☐ e. refuse		☐ a. to discard	☐ d. to dump	
☐ b. book	☐ f. waste		☐ b. to toss away	☐ e. to preserve	
☐ c. trash	☐ g. collection		☐ c. to value	☐ f. to save	
☐ d. sofa	☐ h. scrap				

4. Check (✔) the items that are frequently imported or exported.

☐ a. animals   ☐ e. furniture

☐ b. cars   ☐ f. food

☐ c. clothing   ☐ g. plants

☐ d. trash   ☐ h. music

2 | Active Previewing

A. Preview the online article on the next page and tell a partner two things you remember about it.

B. Work as a class or in large groups. Try to name as many things as you can about the text.

C. Then answer these questions with a partner.

1. What is the topic of this text?

2. What is the most important thing the author wants you to know about the topic?

> **REMEMBER**
>
> Preview online articles by reading the title, subtitles, the first sentence of every paragraph, and the last sentence of the text. For more about *previewing online articles*, see page 3.

3 | Reading and Recalling

A. Read the text. Stop after each paragraph and tell a partner two things that you remember about it.

China is Talking Trash

China has recognized the value of trash and is buying as much U.S. refuse as it can get its hands on. *The Wall Street Journal* related[1] this illustrative[2] tale.

1   In late February, nine-year-old Kevin Sayad finished a two-page homework assignment on fractions. After he went over it with his fourth-grade teacher and reviewed it with his parents, he discarded the homework at his New Jersey home. But that wasn't the end of the line for the boy's homework. When he tossed out that piece of paper, Kevin was actually tossing in a small contribution to the trade between two economic giants, the U.S. and China.

2   Kevin's scrap ended up in a Clifton, N.J. recycling plant on 5 March. There, it was dumped into a giant green paper baler, shoved with 1,500 pounds of other paper into a rectangular jumble3 bound by thick steel wire, and stuffed into a shipping container destined for Ningbo, a port city on China's eastern seaboard. In China, the boy's discarded homework will sell to a paper mill that gobbles up America's throwaways and spits out new paper products.

3   American exports to China are booming in an unlikely area: junk. Every year, tons of metal from discarded cars and old household appliances, paper from empty cardboard boxes and crumpled newspapers, and plastic from dumped soda bottles are processed, piled onto ships, and sent across the ocean. There they become the raw material for paper mills, steel mills, and other factories, feeding China's fast-growing, import-oriented industrial economy.

4   In 2002, the U.S. exported waste and scrap to China with an estimated value of $1.2 billion, up from $194 million five years earlier, according to Commerce Department data. Scrap is now the nation's third largest export to China, after airplanes and semiconductors and ahead of soybeans and computers. "We are the Saudi Arabia of scrap," says Robert Garino, director of commodity research at the Washington-based Institute of Scrap Recycling Industries. China has become the biggest customer for America's junk, buying 23% of the $5.2 billion in scrap and waste exports.

5   The trade in scrap offers a look into the complex dynamics between the world's largest economy, the U.S., and the world's fastest growing economy, China. Because Americans are buying so much more from China than they sell there, the trade deficit[4] with China is exploding. In 2002, it rose 24% to $103 billion, the largest in history. Yet, despite the huge gap, U.S. exports to China are growing as well. In the same year, they were up 15% to $22 billion, increasing for everything from semiconductors to machine tools to oranges, and even

continued

---

[1] **to relate:** to tell

[2] **illustrative:** clarifying; explained through examples

[3] **jumble:** many things in a state of disorder

[4] **trade deficit:** occurs when the value of a nation's imports is greater than its exports

continued

to scrap and waste. In 2002, one company, America Chung Nam Inc., sold China scrap from the U.S. equal to the weight of 17 aircraft carriers.

6 Some see the scrap trade as an example of the global economy at its most efficient. The U.S., which consumes far more than any other nation, turns out a huge amount of waste. China, with a growing industrial base and a dearth[5] of natural resources such as pulp or iron ore, needs the raw materials.

_____

[5] **dearth:** not enough of something

B. Read the text again without pausing. Tell your partner two new pieces of information that you remember.

C. Work as a class or in large groups. Try to name as many things as you can about the text.

4 | Understanding the Text

A. Answer as many questions as you can without looking at the text. Discuss your answers with a partner.

1. Why did Kevin Sayad's homework go to China? _____

_____

_____

2. What is the relationship between the U.S. and China? _____

_____

_____

3. What does China do with the scrap? _____

_____

_____

B. Write *T* for *True* and *F* for *False* according to the text. If the statement is false, correct it. Discuss your answers with a partner.

___F___ 1. In 2002, the U.S. exported ~~agricultural products~~ worth approximately $1.2 billion. _waste and scrap_

_____ 2. Every year, tons of metal, paper, and plastic are processed and shipped across the ocean to paper mills, steel mills, and other factories in China.

_____

_____ 3. Saudi Arabia sells scrap to China. _____

_____ 4. The U.S. has become the biggest customer for China's junk.

_____

_____ 5. China does not have enough raw materials, such as iron ore.

_____

The **main idea** of a text or paragraph is the most important idea the writer gives about the topic of that text or paragraph. The main idea is always expressed as a complete sentence. To identify the main idea:

1. Choose the idea closest to the most important idea of the whole paragraph or text.

2. Do not choose an idea that is too general.

3. Do not choose an idea that focuses on a specific detail of the paragraph or text.

Reread ¶3 on page 45. The topic is: *U.S. junk as an export to China.* The possible choices for the main idea are:

    a.   American exports to China are booming.

    b.   Every year, tons of plastic from dumped soda bottles are sent to China.

    c.   Junk has become an important U.S. export to China.

Choice *a* is too general. It refers to all American exports, not junk.

Choice *b* is too specific. Plastic is only one kind of junk export mentioned in the paragraph.

Choice *c* is the best main idea for ¶3.

5 | Understanding the Topic and Main Idea

A. Text. Answer the questions and write *T* for *Topic* or *MI* for *Main Idea, G* for *Too General*, and *S* for *Too Specific*. Discuss your answers with a partner.

1. What is the topic of the text?

    a. _____ Kevin Sayad's homework as a scrap export to China

    b. _____ exports to China

    c. _____ U.S. scrap exports to China

2. Is your answer for the topic of the text the same as the one you determined after you previewed the text, or is your answer different? _____

3. What is the main idea of the text?

    a. _____ Exports to China are increasing in a number of areas.

    b. _____ Kevin Sayad's homework is a small contribution to the trade between the U.S. and China.

    c. _____ Every year, the United States exports tons of scrap to China, where it becomes raw material for China's growing industrial economy.

B. Paragraphs. Write *T* for *Topic* or *MI* for *Main Idea*, *G* for *Too General*, and *S* for *Too Specific*. Discuss your answers with a partner.

1. What is the topic for ¶**4**?

    a. _____ U.S. exports to China

    b. _____ scrap as a U.S. export to China

    c. _____ the estimated value of U.S. exported scrap to China

2. What is the main idea for ¶**4**?

    a. _____ Scrap is now the United States' third largest export to China.

    b. _____ The U.S. exports many different goods to China.

    c. _____ The U.S. exported an estimated $1.2 billion in scrap to China in 2002.

3. What is the topic for ¶**5**?

    a. _____ the economic dynamics between the U.S. and China

    b. _____ the explosion of the U.S. trade deficit with China

    c. _____ economics

4. What is the main idea for ¶**5**?

    a. _____ Economics is an important issue.

    b. _____ The economic dynamics between the U.S. and China are complex.

    c. _____ The United States' trade deficit with China is growing because Americans are buying more from China than they are selling.

5. What is the topic for ¶**6**?

    a. _____ the waste produced by the U.S.

    b. _____ the efficiency of the scrap trade

    c. _____ the global economy

6. What is the main idea for ¶**6**?

    a. _____ The scrap trade is seen as an example of the global economy at its most efficient.

    b. _____ The global economy is efficient.

    c. _____ The United States consumes more than any other nation and produces a huge amount of waste.

Phrasal verbs are verbs combined with particles like *in, out, up, down, through, over,* and *onto*. When a verb is combined with a particle, it can have a different meaning from the verb and/or particle by itself. Use the surrounding context to help you understand the meaning of phrasal verbs.

Read the following sentence.

After he *went over* [his homework] with his fourth-grade teacher and reviewed it with his parents, he discarded the homework at his New Jersey home. (¶2)

The verb *go* generally indicates movement. However, in this case, the fourth-grader does not really move himself over his homework. We know that children examine or review their homework with their teachers and parents. The verb *to go* plus the particle *over* together make a phrasal verb that means *to evaluate, to review,* or *to examine.*

6 | Understanding Vocabulary in Context—Phrasal Verbs

Match each phrasal verb with its definition. Discuss your answers with a partner.

_____ 1. to toss out (¶1)

_____ 2. to toss in (¶1)

_____ 3. to end up (¶2)

_____ 4. to pile onto (¶3)

_____ 5. to turn out (¶6)

a. to produce

b. to contribute

c. to arrive at a destination

d. to put something in the trash

e. to place on in large quantities or numbers

7 | Discussing the Issues

Answer the questions and discuss your answers with a partner.

1. According to the text, "some see the scrap trade as an example of the global economy at its most efficient." Do you agree or disagree? Why?

2. Do you think the U.S. could benefit from recycling more of its own scrap? Why or why not?

3. What do you think would be the most profitable kind of scrap to recycle, and why?

Text 2 | Curb Appeal

1 | Getting Started

A. Answer the questions and briefly discuss your answers with a partner.

1. Have you ever put something on the street for someone else to take?

2. Have you ever found anything on the street that you liked and kept?

3. What happens to things after you discard them?

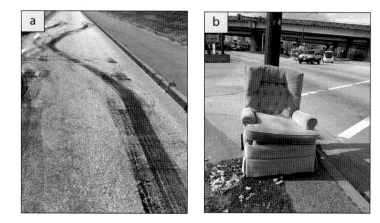

4. Check (✔) all of the words or phrases that could describe photo *a*.

☐ a. curb

☐ b. curbside

☐ c. the side of the road

☐ d. parking lot

☐ e. street

☐ f. storefront

5. Look at photo *b*. What other unwanted items could people leave on the street?

B. Complete the chart. Write three things you could or should do with each item. Discuss your answers with a partner.

An old pair of jeans with a hole in the knee	Old magazines	A lock without a combination
1.	1.	1.
2.	2.	2.
3.	3.	3.

2 | Active Previewing

A. Preview the newspaper article below by reading the first two paragraphs. Then with a partner, answer as many questions as you can without looking at the text.

1. **Who** (what group of people) is discussed in this text?

2. **What** do they do?

3. **Where** do they do it?

4. **When** do they do it?

B. Work as a class or in large groups. Try to name as many things as you can about the text.

C. Then answer the questions with a partner.

1. What is the topic of this text?

2. What is the main idea of this text?

REMEMBER

Preview newspaper articles by reading the title and any captions, looking at any photos, and reading the first two to four paragraphs. For more on *previewing newspaper articles*, see page 28.

3 | Reading and Recalling

A. Read the text. Stop after each paragraph and tell a partner two things that you remember about it.

Curb Appeal

BY JAN UEBELHERR

1 **Trash or Treasure**

One person's trash is another person's treasure when it comes to making finds on the streets. Carpets, a mink stole, cashmere[1] sweaters, a piano, and a marble-top coffee table. Marylyn Kruger just can't understand it.

2 "I don't know why people throw these things out," Kruger says of the things she has pulled from the side of the road. "I can drive around on a Saturday and go rummaging and not spend a cent." Weekends are a favorite time to go collecting.

3 Kruger is one of a legion[2] of curbside hunters and pickers, always alert to the things that have been cast aside by others.

4 Kruger can offer a quick course in what all such treasure hunters know. There are four keys to success, she says: "Luck, timing, weather, and transportation of items."

5 The first, luck, is self-explanatory. Timing means being there when luck strikes and acting fast. Good weather keeps things in good shape until one finds them. Having the right wheels makes getting things home a lot easier. For example, a minivan or SUV works better than, say, a bike.

6 "I'm lucky. I have a convertible," Kruger says.

7 Here are some noteworthy stories of cast-offs reclaimed by curbside treasure hunters.

continued

---

[1] **cashmere:** a soft, luxurious wool made from the fleece of a Kashmir goat
[2] **legion:** a very large number

8 No Curbing Marylyn

Let's start with the high-ticket items, like the mink and the cashmere sweaters. Kruger found the mink just sitting there in a zippered bag. The cashmere sweaters were in a box.

9   "I happened to look in," she says. "They're so soft; they're 100% cashmere. One has a label in it that says 'Harrods of London®.'"

10   "The biggest and best find has to be the piano. Some men had just put it at the curb. They said that they'd been hired to clear out a house and toss everything." She asked if she could have the piano and they said sure, go ahead. She pondered[3] just how to get it home, offering to pay them to take it to her house, just around the corner on the east side, but they declined.

11   "So I ran home, and luckily, we had a sturdy garden cart on wheels, so my son and husband brought the cart to the piano and pushed it home," she says.

12   "I play my piano every day and always get compliments from people who come to my home and see it for the first time, and I love to tell them how I got it."

13 Give and Take and Give Again

Karen Carnabucci of Racine calls herself an "urban archaeologist." She loves the idea of "finding treasure in trash." A creative arts therapist, she uses found items in her work—beads, pencils, silk flowers, magazines, toys, glittery decorations.

14   Carnabucci has even pulled household items from discarded piles and donated them to charities, such as organizations that serve the poor, the homeless, and runaways.

15   Her best find was a 1943 Green Bay Packers game program, tossed by a neighbor. She donated it to a nonprofit auction and it raised $70.

16 One Man, One TV

Ronald Kutnyak found a television in a driveway just put out by a neighbor in New Berlin. Kutnyak went home and got his wife. They looked it over and asked the neighbor what was wrong with the TV.

17   "He says, 'It shuts off,'" Kutnyak says. "The man had spent $300 two years earlier to fix it and didn't want to spend more." Kutnyak and his son loaded it onto a truck and got it home. A friend who works on audiovisual equipment, such as stereos and TVs, told Kutnyak to remove a panel and check for dust. Kutnyak says he found an inch of dust, which he removed with a brush and a vacuum cleaner. "I plugged it in, ran it for two days in my garage," he says. "The TV never shut off." Other finds: stereo components, vacuum cleaners, bicycles and a safe (the owner had lost the combination; Kutnyak is getting a replacement from the manufacturer).

18   "I go rummaging on Tuesdays and Fridays, when the garbage collection is," he says. "This is a throwaway society, and people don't realize what they're throwing away."

19 A Mom with a Mission

Stephanie Erbes lived in Portland, Ore., for four years, and she has traveled the world, but she believes Milwaukee has an especially tempting array of curbside castoffs.

20   Her family jokes that most of her stuff comes from "the side of the road," and she figures they're probably right. A single mom with 3 1/2-year-old twins, she's always looking to save money.

21   So far, Erbes has been able to get lots of stuff for the twins this way. All of their beds, with the exception of their first bassinets[4], were found

continued

---

[4] **bassinet:** a small, portable crib for a bab

[3] **to ponder:** to think about, to reflect

on the side of the road. She's also picked up ride-on toys, child-sized chairs, and other items for them.

22   Erbes has found and taken home rugs, outdoor tables and benches, a Singer® sewing machine, and a push lawn mower. One of her favorite finds is a vintage[5] Underwood® type writer. "Still functions, no broken parts," she says.

23   Another neighbor noticed Erbes' habit of street shopping and came to her door and said, "I'm wondering if you'd like to take a walk through my place and take what you want—as I notice most of it is ending up over here anyway."

[5] **vintage:** classic, old

B. Read the text again without pausing. Tell your partner two new pieces of information that you remember.

C. Work as a class or in large groups. Try to name as many things as you can about the text.

4 | Understanding the Text

A. Answer as many questions as you can without looking at the text. Discuss your answers with a partner.

1. According to Marylyn Kruger, what are the four keys to treasure-hunting success?

_____

_____

2. What is one way Karen Carnabucci makes use of her curbside finds?

_____

_____

3. What is one way curbside finds have helped Stephanie Erbes? _____

_____

B. Check (✔) all of the items that were curbside finds, according to the text.

☐ a. a mink stole

☐ b. a computer

☐ c. a priceless oil painting

☐ d. a television

☐ e. a piano

☐ f. a kitchen sink

☐ g. cashmere sweaters

☐ h. a vintage typewriter

5 | Understanding the Topic and Main Idea

Text. Write *T* for *Topic* or *MI* for *Main Idea*, *G* for *Too General*, and *S* for *Too Specific*. Discuss your answers with a partner.

1. What is the topic of the text?

   a. _____ how Marylyn Kruger finds treasures in trash

   b. _____ curbside treasure hunters

   c. _____ life in a throwaway society

2. What is the main idea of the text?

   a. _____ Curbside treasure hunters find a variety of valuable items among things that have been discarded by others.

   b. _____ America is a throwaway society.

   c. _____ Marylyn Kruger has found a variety of treasures by looking through her neighbors' trash.

3. Are your answers for the topic and the main idea the same as the ones you determined after you previewed the text, or are your answers different? _____

   _____

VOCABULARY STRATEGY Understanding Vocabulary in Context—
Examples

Examples often explain unfamiliar words in a text. Examples are given with phrases like *for example, such as,* and *like,* or sometimes they follow a colon (:).

Read the following sentences.

1. Having the right *wheels* makes getting things home a lot easier. For example, a minivan or SUV works better than, say, a bike. (¶5)

   What are *wheels*? The phrase *for example* in the second sentence indicates that *a minivan, SUV,* and *a bike* are examples of *wheels.* We can guess that *wheels* means *a form of transportation that has wheels.*

2. Carnabucci has even pulled household items from discarded piles and donated them to *charities,* such as organizations that serve the poor, the homeless, and runaways. (¶14)

   What are *charities*? The phrase *such as* indicates that *organizations that serve the poor, the homeless, and runaways* are examples of *charities.* We can guess that *charities* means *organizations that help people.*

6 | Understanding Vocabulary in Context

A. Examples. Use examples from the text to help you write a definition for each of the words and phrases.

1. high-ticket item (¶8) _____

2. audiovisual equipment (¶17) _____

3. find (¶17) _____

B. Context Clues. Select the best meaning for each word or phrase according to the text.

1. to go rummaging (¶2, ¶18)

   a. to go shopping

   b. to go out for lunch

   c. to go looking for something

2. to toss (¶10)

   a. to give

   b. to keep

   c. to throw away

3. to decline (¶10)

   a. to refuse or say no

   b. to agree

   c. to throw away

4. throwaway (¶18)

   a. lost

   b. wasteful

   c. valuable

5. castoffs (¶19)

   a. something new

   b. discarded items

   c. pickers

7 | Discussing the Issues

Answer the questions and discuss your answers with a partner.

1. Do you think Stephanie Erbes' neighbor was serious when she offered to let Erbes walk through her place and take what she wanted? Why or why not?

2. Do you think it's normal or strange to throw something away that is still in usable condition? Why?

3. What is your opinion about collecting discarded items from the curbside, as described in this text?

Text 3 | Simple Actions, Real Results

1 | Getting Started

Answer the questions and briefly discuss your answers with a partner.

1. Do you recycle anything?

2. What are two reasons recycling can be important?

3. Which do you think has a better effect on the environment: *preventing* or *recycling* waste? Why?

2 | Active Previewing

Preview the table on the next page, and then answer the questions. Discuss your answers with a partner.

1. What is the title of the table?

2. Check (✔) the two actions that are recommended in the table.

  ☐ a. removing   ☐ d. adding

  ☐ b. causing   ☐ e. recycling

  ☐ c. preventing

3. What is the topic of this table?

> **REMEMBER**
>
> Preview the table by reading the title, the column and/or row headers, and any **boldfaced** information. For more about *previewing tables*, see page 11.

Simple Actions, Real Results

Waste reduction can significantly reduce GHG emissions. Each individual action—from double-sided printing to recycling a soda can—contributes to real GHG reductions. This chart demonstrates the results of reusing or recycling everyday materials.

Preventing 500 tons of...	Equals a reduction of...	Which is approximately equivalent to removing this many cars from the road for one year
Paper	402 MTCE	307 cars
Aluminum	1,247 MTCE	952 cars
Glass	68 MTCE	52 cars
HDPE	244 MTCE	186 cars
Corrugated cardboard	257 MTCE	196 cars

Recycling 500 tons of...	Equals a reduction of...	Which is approximately equivalent to removing this many cars from the road for one year
Paper	339 MTCE	259 cars
Aluminum	2,055 MTCE	1,569 cars
Glass	38 MTCE	29 cars
HDPE	192 MTCE	147 cars
Corrugated cardboard	354 MTCE	270 cars

Abbreviations:
GHG – Greenhouse Gas   HDPE – High Density Polyethylene   MTCE – Metric Tons of Carbon Equivalent

3 | Scanning

Scan the table for the answers to the questions. Discuss your answers with a partner.

1. What does MTCE stand for? _____

2. What is the abbreviation for "greenhouse gas"? _____

3. Preventing 500 tons of glass is approximately equivalent to removing how many cars from the road for one year? _____

4. Recycling 500 tons of aluminum is approximately equivalent to removing how many cars from the road for one year? _____

5. Preventing 500 tons of paper equals a reduction of how many MTCE?

_____

6. Recycling 500 tons of what equals a reduction of 354 MTCE?

_____

7. Which has a greater benefit: preventing or recycling 500 tons of glass?

_____

8. Which has a greater benefit: preventing or recycling 500 tons of aluminum?

_____

REMEMBER

Scan the table by reading quickly and stopping only for related words and symbols. For more about *scanning*, see page 12.

4 | Discussing the Issues

Answer the questions and discuss your answers with a partner.

1. Do you think governments should get involved in people's recycling efforts? Why or why not?

2. What are two ways towns and cities can encourage their citizens to reuse and recycle?

3. What do you know about greenhouse gas? How is it affecting the ozone layer?

Text 4 | Building Tires

1 | Getting Started

A. Answer the questions and briefly discuss your answers with a partner.

1. Are people in your city or area concerned about the environment?

2. What are three environmental problems that you think affect the world today?

3. What are three possible solutions to these environmental problems?

B. Check (✔) all of the practical uses for scrap tires, like the tires shown in the photo.

Scrap tires could be used...	
☐ a. in house construction.	☐ f. as fuel.
☐ b. for clothing.	☐ g. to make shoes.
☐ c. as food.	☐ h. as computer equipment.
☐ d. in playgrounds.	☐ i. in highway construction.
☐ e. to make dams or fences.	☐ j. as new tires.

scrap tires

2 | Active Previewing

A. Preview the academic text on the next page and tell a partner two things you remember about it.

B. Work as a class or in large groups. Try to name as many things as you can about the text.

C. Then answer these questions with a partner.

1. What is the topic of this text?

2. What is the main idea of this text?

> **REMEMBER**
> Preview academic texts by reading the title, the first sentence of each paragraph, the final sentence of the text, and by looking at photos and captions.
> For more about *previewing academic texts,* see page 3.

3 | Reading and Recalling

A. Read the text. Stop after each paragraph and tell a partner two things that you remember about it.

Building Tires

One UA Researcher Has High Hopes
for Scrap Tires

by David Barber

1   Adjunct Professor Emeritus Stuart Hoenig, of the University of Arizona's department of agriculture and biosystems engineering, thinks he is on to the next wave in building materials: used tires. While Hoenig is especially interested in their use for building houses, he is testing out a number of uses for these discarded tires.

2   Hoenig has been at the University of Arizona (UA) since 1973. Although he is already retired and thus no longer teaches, he stays on at the University to pursue research. One of the projects he is pursuing with scrap tires is in landscaping and gardening.

3   The University of Arizona is currently monitoring one of Hoenig's demonstration projects on campus. "You split the tire like a bagel, then you roll the grass back, put the tires down, fill them with dirt, and roll the grass back," explains Hoenig, a national expert in the use of scrap tires. "It uses about 50 percent less water and the grass looks great." In fact, the University of Arizona is acting as an agent for a California colleague who has patented[1] this use of split tires to save water.

4   One of the reasons the UA and other universities have been studying engineering applications for these scrap tires is to offer environmental solutions to a growing problem. There are some 500 million used tires stockpiled[2] in the U.S., with a growth rate equal to about 250 million per year, creating hazards, such as fire and environmental risks. When they are placed in landfills, they tend to rise to the surface, which has caused 33 states to forbid their landfill placement altogether.

5   Currently nine states allow the use of whole tires for the construction of dams, erosion control, houses, fencing, rifle range bullet stops, bridge supports, terracing, playgrounds, and grain storage structures. With an expected life span of some 20 years, they are an economical substitute for traditional building materials, like concrete, steel, and wood. In 2000, the nation used 32 million scrap tires (the amount generated annually in California alone) in civil engineering projects, up by 28 percent from 1999. This made it the second largest end use for scrap tires in the nation.

6   At present, the largest end use for scrap tires is tire-derived fuel (TDF). The tires are broken down into small chips and burned by power plants in order to create energy. However, the ovens that burn the chips are costly.

7   Another use for the tires is as bedding for livestock, such as cows and sheep. The bedding allows liquid to drain, keeping the animals drier and preventing foot diseases. California Polytechnic State University, San Luis Obispo, has built a huge system of livestock bedding. Although the UA's Agriculture farm isn't "officially" using the technique, Hoenig is trying to get the funds to pursue such a project.

8   There is also a great variety of applications for scrap tires in home building. "The big thing is house construction; the installation is fantastic," says Hoenig, and scrap tires are free. Hoenig feels that building inexpensive homes with tires would be great for poorer areas and notes that the construction doesn't take any special skills. What he and other scrap tire supporters are hoping for is that home builders and subcontractors become more aware of the uses for scrap tires.

House made of recycled material

9   It is the use of whole tires that has drawn Hoenig's interest, as they can be "baled." Baling

continued

---

[1] **to patent:** to obtain the sole right to make, use, or sell an invention for a certain period of time
[2] **to stockpile:** to accumulate

continued

is a process in which a loose material, such as cotton or hay, is tightly bound together with wire or cord. The finished product is highly compact. Tires can be compacted, too. In fact, there are a number of companies all over the U.S. that bale tires, and Hoenig notes that there is one company that actually produces a square tire bale, ideal for building.

10   The baled tires are used for the walls in various structures, such as dams, fences, and houses, where they are stacked, tightly filled with earth, and covered with stucco. All the structures are solid, and houses built from baled tires are even well insulated and resistant to fire and insects.

11   Seasonal flooding in the southwest can cause streambeds to drop ten feet a year, which can create big problems, especially for the ranchers. Tires, in the form of retaining walls, are being used to reduce the damage and slow the flow of rushing water. Furthermore, dams constructed with baled tires cost 60 percent less than a concrete dam.

12   Hoenig and his University colleagues are responsible for the construction of a tire bale dam at a ranch nearby. They stacked and tied together the tires with half-inch plastic straps, filled them with gravel, and covered them with chain-link mesh.

13   The 30-foot-long, six-foot-high tire dam was monitored by the Arizona Department of Environmental Quality and cost about $6,500 to design—about $63,000 less than a comparable concrete dam. The 1,200 tires were free, and Pima County probationers supplied the free labor. The dam has stopped sand some five feet deep and 30 feet wide from being lost into the arroyo. "The ranchers were very dubious[3] of it at the time," notes Hoenig. "But it's four years later and it has withstood[4] two floods. Now they're convinced."

14   In fact, the ranchers in the area are so convinced that they are eager for more dams. "They'd all like to have tire dams because they're cheap and they work well," says Hoenig. "Right now, we're trying to get some money to build more tire dams."

15   Although Hoenig is already in charge of a great number of projects, he's recently received a proposal to create a 100,000-gallon anaerobic digester. Anaerobic digestion is a process that uses bacteria to break down organic matter, such as food scraps, grass cuttings, leaves, paper—anything that is made from a plant or animal. The growing garbage dumps around the University are looking for solutions to control the excess garbage. Hoenig is planning to use scrap tires to line the site.

16   Around the country, there are many other scrap tire construction projects. For example, the U.S. Department of Interior has used whole tires for 20 years at the Salton Sea for erosion and dams. In New Mexico, a 4,400-foot section of Lake Carlsbad was stabilized[5] against erosion with tire bales. In this case the bales were covered with a thin layer of concrete for aesthetic purposes. More than 50,000 tires were used to build a 25-foot-high dam in Arkansas. California used 860,000 tires to fill in a freeway embankment. In Maryland, scrap tires have been used for playground structures and ground cover in seven state parks. Clearly, some people are beginning to see the benefits of using scrap tires in a number of different ways.

17   The uses for scrap tires are varied and effective. Furthermore, their use presents a creative solution for the growing problem of what to do with old tires, which otherwise present significant environmental and fire hazards in our communities.

---

[3] **dubious:** doubtful; undecided
[4] **to withstand:** to resist successfully
[5] **to stabilize:** to make stable or fixed

B. Read the text again without pausing. Tell your partner two new pieces of information that you remember.

C. Work as a class or in large groups. Try to name as many things as you can about the text.

4 | Understanding the Text

A. Answer as many questions as you can without looking at the text. Discuss your answers with a partner.

1. Who is Professor Hoenig? _____

2. Why is the University of Arizona studying applications for scrap tires? _____

_____

_____

3. What is a growing problem with scrap tires in the U.S.? _____

_____

_____

4. What are two uses for tires in construction? _____

_____

_____

5. What do the ranchers near the University of Arizona think about scrap tires? _____

_____

B. Complete the chart with uses for scrap tires, and the advantage of each use, according to the text.

Use	Advantage
1.	
2.	
3.	

5 | Understanding the Topic and Main Idea

A. Text. Write *T* for *Topic* or *MI* for *Main Idea*, *G* for *Too General*, and *S* for *Too Specific*. Discuss your answers with a partner.

1. What is the topic of the text?

    a. _____ houses made from scrap tires

    b. _____ construction projects

    c. _____ the uses for scrap tires

2. What is the main idea of the text?

    a. _____ The uses for scrap tires are varied and offer an economical solution to a growing environmental problem.

    b. _____ Houses made from scrap tires are economical, well insulated, and resistant to fire and insects.

    c. _____ Construction projects are increasing in number around the world.

3. Are your answers for the topic and the main idea the same as the ones you determined after you previewed the text, or are your answers different? Explain. _____

_____

B. Paragraphs. Write *T* for *Topic* or *MI* for *Main Idea, G* for *Too General*, and *S* for *Too Specific.* Discuss your answers with a partner.

1. What is the topic for ¶**4**?

    a. _____ 500 million used tires in the U.S.

    b. _____ the growing environmental problem of scrap tires

    c. _____ environmental problems in the U.S.

2. What is the main idea for ¶**4**?

    a. _____ Scrap tires are increasing in number annually and pose a serious environmental threat in the U.S.

    b. _____ There are many environmental problems in the U.S. that require solutions.

    c. _____ There are around 500 million used tires in the U.S.

3. What is the topic for ¶**8**?

    a. _____ home construction

    b. _____ using scrap tires in home construction

    c. _____ no special skills needed for scrap tire home construction

4. What is the main idea for ¶**8**?

    a. _____ Using scrap tires for home construction doesn't require any special skills.

    b. _____ Scrap tires can be used in a number of ways in home construction and are an inexpensive option.

    c. _____ House construction is important.

5. What is the topic for ¶**16**?

    a. _____ dams built with scrap tires in the U.S.

    b. _____ the uses for scrap tires

    c. _____ scrap tire construction projects in the U.S.

6. What is the main idea for ¶**16**?

    a. _____ Many dams around the U.S. have been built with scrap tires.

    b. _____ There is a great variety of uses for scrap tires.

    c. _____ Around the U.S. there are many construction projects that have used scrap tires as part of their materials.

6 | Understanding Vocabulary in Context

A. **Examples.** Use examples from the text to help you write a definition for each of the words and phrases.

1. hazard (¶4) *fire and environmental risk; dangerous thing*

2. traditional building material(s) (¶5) _____

3. livestock (¶7) _____

4. organic matter (¶15) _____

B. **Context Clues.** Match each word or phrase on the left with the best definition on the right according to the text.

_____ 1. the next wave (¶1)   a. lifetime

_____ 2. to monitor (¶3, ¶13)   b. to be pressed together tightly

_____ 3. erosion (¶5, ¶16)   d. the new way

_____ 4. life span (¶5)   c. related to appearance

_____ 5. to be compacted (¶9)   e. wearing away

_____ 6. aesthetic (¶16)   f. to observe

7 | Discussing the Issues

Answer the questions and discuss your answers with a partner.

1. Which of the uses for scrap tires is the most beneficial or effective? Why?

2. According to Hoenig, scrap tires are wonderful for housing construction. Would you like to live in a house made of scrap tires? Why or why not?

3. Could it be difficult to persuade more engineers and house builders to use scrap tires in their projects? Why or why not?

Putting It On Paper

A. Write a three-paragraph essay on one of these topics.

1. Do you think that recycling is a good idea for you to practice? Compare and contrast the advantages and disadvantages of starting a personal recycling program.

2. Do you think governments should invest money in recycling projects for communities? Compare and contrast the advantages and disadvantages.

Steps for your essay

a. In your first paragraph, clearly state your opinion about the topic. Give reasons.

b. In your second paragraph, compare and contrast several advantages and disadvantages of the topic you have chosen.

c. In your final paragraph, restate your opinion about the topic and the reason(s) for your opinion.

B. Exchange essays with a partner. First, read your partner's essay and answer the questions in the checklist. Then give feedback to your partner.

✓ CHECKLIST
1. Does ¶1 show your partner's opinion about the topic?
2. Does ¶2 show the advantages and disadvantages of your partner's topic?
3. Does ¶3 restate your partner's opinion about the topic and his or her reason(s) why?
4. Are you persuaded by your partner's ideas?
5. Is there any information in the essay that is not related to the topic your partner chose? If yes, please underline it on your partner's paper, and write it below:

_____

_____

_____

_____

_____

_____

_____

C. Revise your essay based on your partner's feedback.

Taking It Online | The Three "Rs"

A. With a partner, use the Internet to research ideas on reducing, reusing, and recycling.

1. Use Google (www.google.com) or another major search engine to begin your online research.

2. Search for websites with information about recycling or reusing the three old items in the chart below. (Try typing "recycling" or "reusing" and the name of the item in the search field.)

3. Preview the websites.

ONLINE TIP

Most search engines have features that allow you to search for Images, News, Audio, and Video.

B. Complete the table with the information you find.

Aluminum or tin cans
Name:
Website address:
Recycling or reuse idea:

Old socks
Name:
Website address:
Recycling or reuse idea:

Old cell phones (mobile phones)
Name:
Website address:
Recycling or reuse idea:

C. Following up. With your partner, think of another way to recycle or reuse each of the items above. Discuss your ideas with the class, and have a class or group vote on the best idea.

Uncovering History

Answer the questions and briefly discuss your answers with a partner.

1. Are there any famous historical or archaeological sites in your city or country?

2. Look at the photos and try to identify what you see. Have you ever been to any sites like these or seen any artifacts?

3. Do you think it is important to preserve historical sites? Why or why not?

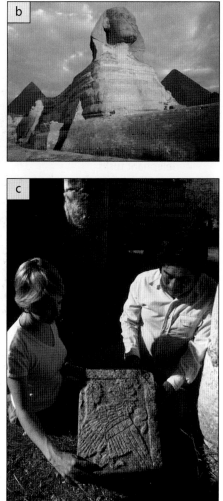

Text 1 | Stealing History

1 | Getting Started

A. Answer the questions and briefly discuss your answers with a partner.

1. Look at the photos. Circle all of the items that are illegal to import or export.

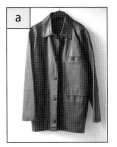
a leather coat

a tiger skin

perfume

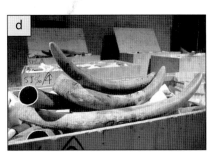
elephant tusks

artifacts

2. What other items can you think of that are illegal to import or export?

3. Why is it illegal to import or export these items?

B. Check (✔) if you think the person is *guilty* or *not guilty* of a crime. Briefly discuss your answers with a partner.

A person . . .	Guilty	Not guilty
1. …knowingly brings an illegal item into/out of a country.	☐	☐
2. …unknowingly brings an illegal item into/out of a country.	☐	☐
3. …buys something old and unique from a market without asking the seller where the item came from.	☐	☐
4. …knowingly brings an illegal item into/out of a country, but plans to give the item to a museum.	☐	☐
5. …is caught bringing an illegal item out of a country, but claims that he/she did not know the item was in his/her suitcase.	☐	☐

2 | Active Previewing

A. Preview the newspaper article below by reading the first two paragraphs. Then answer these questions with a partner.

1. **Who** is the main subject of this article?

2. **What** did he attempt to do?

3. **Where** did the artifacts come from?

4. **When** was he sentenced?

B. Work as a class or in large groups. Try to name as many things as you can about the text.

C. Then answer these questions with a partner.

1. What is the topic of this text?

2. What is the main idea of this text?

REMEMBER

Preview newspaper articles by reading the title and any captions, looking at any photos, and reading the first two to four paragraphs. For more on *previewing newspaper articles*, see page 28.

3 | Reading and Recalling

A. Read the text. Stop after each paragraph and tell a partner two things that you remember about it.

Alumnus Admits Smuggling Iraqi Artifacts

BY HANNAH CHARLICK

1   Middle Eastern expert and Princeton graduate alumnus Joseph Braude was sentenced Monday for attempting to smuggle into the United States some 4,000-year-old artifacts that had been looted, or illegally taken, from the Iraqi National Museum.

2   Braude was sentenced to six months under house arrest and two years' probation[1] after pleading guilty[2] of smuggling and making false statements before U.S. District Judge Allyne Ross in August.

3   Braude studied Near Eastern languages at Yale and Arabic and Islamic history at Princeton in the late 1990s. He left the University without completing his doctoral dissertation, according to Kathleen O'Neill, department manager of the Near Eastern studies department. He is fluent in Arabic, Hebrew, and Farsi and has worked effectively with the U.S. government and several news agencies on Middle Eastern affairs and counter-terrorism.

4   Braude, who describes himself as an Iraqi-American, was arrested when going through a routine customs examination at J.F.K. Airport on June 11, 2003. Customs agents there found three marble and alabaster seals[3] in his suitcase that he had not declared to customs when he arrived from London. He also claimed he had not visited Iraq during his trip, according to a statement released by the office of U.S. Attorney Roslynn Mauskopf.

5   The marble and alabaster seals were marked on the bottom in black ink with the initials "IM" and a serial number. An associate professor of ancient Near Eastern art and archaeology at Columbia University confirmed that the items belonged to

continued

---

[1] **probation:** period during which a criminal is released from jail but still must have regular contact with a government official in order to evaluate his or her conduct

[2] **to plead guilty:** to admit one's guilt in a court of law

[3] **marble and alabaster seals:** objects from the museum; originally used to make a mark on official documents

continued

Iraq's Akkadian period of 2340–2180 B.C.E., according to the statement.

6   Braude later admitted to agents of the Bureau of Immigration and Customs Enforcement that he had bought the seals for $200 on the black market[4] in Baghdad and knew that they had probably been looted from the Iraqi National Museum in April 2003.

7   In a press release from the Justice Department announcing Braude's arrest, Mauskopf stated, "This administration sent a clear signal[5] that we would not allow thieves to take advantage of the conflict in Iraq to pilfer its antiquities."

8   Braude told *The New York Times* that he had visited Iraq in June 2003 to research an introduction to his book *The New Iraq: Rebuilding the Country for Its People, the Middle East and the World,* published last year.

9   According to the report from the customs agents who questioned him, Braude had told agents that he planned to have the seals inspected and then give them "to the proper authorities."

---

[4] **black market:** a place where one can buy illegal or stolen goods
[5] **to send a clear signal:** to make something clearly understood

B. Read the text again without pausing. Tell your partner two new pieces of information that you remember.

C. Work as a class or in large groups. Try to name as many things as you can about the text.

4 | Understanding the Text

A. Answer as many questions as you can without looking at the text. Discuss your answers with a partner.

1. What kind of punishment did Joseph Braude receive for his crime? _____

   _____

2. How did Braude get caught? _____

3. According to Braude, why had he been in Iraq at the time he bought the seals? _____

   _____

B. Complete the chart. First, indicate where each event occurred by writing *Iraq* or *U.S.* in the Location column. Then put the events in order by numbering them *1* through *5* in the Sequence column.

Event	Location	Sequence
1. Braude researched the introduction to his book.	Iraq	
2. Braude studied Near Eastern languages.		1
3. Braude told agents he planned to have the seals inspected.		
4. Braude was arrested.		
5. Braude was sentenced to six months under house arrest.		
6. Braude bought some objects stolen from the Iraqi museum.		

5 | Understanding the Topic and Main Idea

Text. Answer the questions and write *MI* for *Main Idea,* *G* for *Too General,* and *S* for *Too Specific*. Discuss your answers with a partner.

1. What is the topic of the text? _____

2. What is the main idea of the text?

    a. _____ A Princeton alumnus was arrested and sentenced for smuggling artifacts out of Iraq.

    b. _____ Three stone seals were looted from the Iraqi National Museum.

    c. _____ Smuggling of artifacts in Iraq has become a big problem since April 2003.

3. Are your answers for the topic and the main idea the same as the ones you determined after you previewed the text, or are your answers different? _____

Possessive adjectives are like adjectives in that they modify nouns or noun phrases. The *possessive* adjectives are: **my**, **your**, **her**, **his**, **its**, **our**, and **their**. Sometimes, a possessive adjective refers to a noun or noun phrase in the same sentence, and it is easier to see what the possessive adjective refers to. In other cases, the noun or noun phrase might come before or after the possessive adjective (in another sentence), and it is harder to see.

Read the following sentence.

Braude studied Near Eastern languages at Yale and Arabic and Islamic history at Princeton in the late 1990s. He left the University without completing *his* doctoral dissertation... (¶**3**)

Who did not complete *his* doctoral dissertation? If we refer to the sentence that comes before, we can see that the only logical noun or noun phrase is *Braude*. It was *Braude's* doctoral dissertation.

6 | Understanding Possessive Adjectives

Answer the questions and discuss your answers with a partner.

1. In ¶**4**, what do these possessive adjectives refer to?

   a. his (his suitcase) _Braude_____

   b. his (his trip) _____

2. In ¶**7**, what does *its* (its antiquities) refer to? _____

3. In ¶**8**, what do these possessive adjectives refer to?

   a. his (his book) _____

   b. Its (Its People) _____

7 | Understanding Vocabulary in Context—Context Clues

Check (✔) all of the words or phrases that can mean "to take illegally."

1. _____ to smuggle (¶**1**, ¶**2**)   3. _____ to arrest (¶**4**)   5. _____ to pilfer (¶**7**)

2. _____ to loot (¶**1**, ¶**6**)   4. _____ to declare (¶**4**)   6. _____ to inspect (¶**9**)

8 | Discussing the Issues

Answer the questions and discuss your answers with a partner.

1. Why do you think Braude bought the seals if he knew they were stolen?

2. Do you believe what Braude told the customs agents in ¶**9**? Why or why not?

3. Do you think Braude's punishment was fair, too severe, or not severe enough? Why?

Text 2 | Recreating an Army

1 | Getting Started

The Mediterranean Sea

A. Answer the questions and briefly discuss your answers with a partner.

1. Do you like historical movies?

2. Look at the photo. Check (✔) the time period the actors' dress comes from.

    ☐ a. around 330 B.C.E.

    ☐ b. around 1250 A.C.E.

    ☐ c. around 1925 A.C.E.

3. Look at the map. Check (✔) all of the countries that are located in this area of the world.

    ☐ a. Korea   ☐ c. Madagascar   ☐ e. Morocco

    ☐ b. Greece   ☐ d. Macedonia   ☐ f. India

B. Complete the chart with three ways you could research a true event that took place 1,000 years ago. Briefly discuss your answers with a partner.

Ways to research a true event
1. visit a historical site related to the event
2.
3.

2 | Active Previewing

A. Preview the newspaper article below by reading the first two paragraphs. Then answer these questions with a partner.

1. **Who** is Dale Dye?

2. **What** does he do?

3. **When** does the film *Alexander* take place?

B. Work as a class or in large groups. Try to name as many things as you can about the text.

C. Answer the questions with a partner.

1. What is the topic of this text?

2. What is the main idea of this text?

3 | Reading and Recalling

A. Read the text. Stop after each paragraph and tell a partner two things that you remember about it.

Alexander's Army Marches Again

BY HUGH HART

1   LOS ANGELES — Retired Marine Capt. Dale Dye is the technical adviser for *Alexander*, Oliver Stone's biopic about the Macedonian conqueror. The film stars Colin Farrell as Alexander, who died at age 32 after leading his army across 22,000 miles on foot and horseback to vanquish[1] most of the known civilized world around 2,400 years ago.

2   Dye's specialty is assisting directors to create realistic war environments for movies. In 1986, Dye trained actors to behave like military men for Stone's *Platoon.* He did so again for Steven Spielberg's World War II movie *Saving Private Ryan* in 1998. For the first film, Dye was able to use his own experience as a Vietnam veteran, and for the second, he relied on firsthand accounts[2] and archival film footage[3] to make the movies as realistic as possible. In order to recreate the battles for *Alexander*, however, Dye had to use other sources. This time, he turned to the ancient Roman scholars Plutarch, Arrian, Diodorus Siculus, and Quintus Curtius Rufus.

3   But Dye felt something was missing from these sources. "Of course you consult the ancient Roman sources, but there were so many practical questions that were unanswered," says Dye, a white-maned, square-jawed 60-year-old. He has a firm handshake

continued

---

[1] **to vanquish:** to defeat

[2] **firsthand account:** a report of events told by someone who experienced it

[3] **archival film footage:** old or historical movies

and is so commanding that Farrell spent three weeks in a desert tent with him in order to observe the captain's leadership qualities.

4   "There's been a lot of guessing by academics about how Alexander's army actually fought these battles," Dye says. "I was convinced that in order to find out what really happened, we had to presume[4] that Alexander and his Macedonians had the same sort of soldierly mentality as they do today in Baghdad or anyplace else."

5   In his research, Dye gained new respect for a powerful and effective military formation invented by Alexander's father, King Philip (played by Val Kilmer). Using this formation, called the syntagma, Alexander never lost a battle. Dye claims that no one in modern times had ever tried it. Therefore, he decided to put it together and give the actors the same weapons and battle gear that Alexander's Macedonian soldiers would have had.

6   By actually testing it out, Dye believes he corrected a few misunderstandings. "It took weeks and months of studying this stuff before we put 256 men in a syntagma, including eleven principal actors, and tried it. We were trying to realize Oliver's vision, but what we also did, I think, was that we taught the academics a few things about how it was really done."

7   To prepare his army for the film's big battle scenes, Dye set up tents in the Moroccan desert and subjected cast members and 1,000 Moroccan soldiers to three weeks of extremely hard workouts. "In those days, fighting, to a major extent, was hand to hand. We needed the actors to understand that, and to go through the conditioning of a Macedonian soldier. We worked sunup to sundown.

We cooked our own food, we ate in the field, we lived under canvas out in the desert, and we pushed as hard as we could."

8   This backbreaking training proved necessary in the reenacting[5] of *Alexander's* Battle of Gaugamela. The original battle took place in Iraq near what is now Fallujah, where 47,000 Macedonian soldiers defeated Darius and his Persian army of 250,000. Dye, serving as second unit director, coordinated those battle scenes.

9   "If you look at the Battle of Gaugamela in this movie, those are trained, disciplined soldiers who know what they're doing," Dye says. "We had 1,361 men on the field, 102 horses and ten camels, four war chariots, and we were controlling all of it, moving as a disciplined unit. That's where training pays off." The film's second big action sequence transforms Alexander's two-year military campaign in India into a surreal, 15-minute bloodbath in which the Macedonian army fights Indian soldiers mounted on battle-trained elephants.

10   Stone required his departments to create historically accurate detailing wherever possible. The silver drinking cups seen in the film are exact replicas of ancient goblets discovered in an archaeological dig, while the discovery of what some believe to be King Philip's grave in 1977 gave the makeup department specific cues when it came to transforming Kilmer into a likeness of Alexander's one-eyed father. According to the historical consultant, Kilmer's face is made up to look like the skull found in King Philip's tomb would have looked. Says Fox, "It's perfect, as if Philip came back from the grave."

---

[4] **presume:** to accept as true

[5] **to reenact:** to recreate

B. Read the text again without pausing. Tell your partner two new things that you remember.

C. Work as a class or in large groups. Try to name as many things as you can about the text.

4 | Understanding the Text

A. Answer as many questions as you can without looking at the text. Discuss your answers with a partner.

1. What does Captain Dale Dye do on movie productions? _____

2. How did Dye do the research for *Alexander*? _____

3. What kind of preparation did the actors have for the battle scenes in *Alexander*?

_____

B. Complete the sentences according to the text. Discuss your answers with a partner.

1. For the film, Dye assumed that Alexander and his Macedonians had _____.

   a. the same sort of soldierly mentality as soldiers do today

   b. a different sort of soldierly mentality than soldiers do today

   c. a more disciplined mentality than soldiers do today

2. Alexander's father, King Philip, invented _____.

   a. warfare on horseback   b. the syntagma   c. current-day military discipline

3. By using the syntagma, Alexander _____.

   a. blinded his father   b. never lost a battle   c. didn't have to sleep in the desert

4. In Alexander the Great's time, fighting was to a great extent _____.

   a. hand-to-hand   b. on horseback   c. in the desert

5. The Battle of Gaugamela took place in present-day _____.

   a. India   b. Greece   c. Iraq

5 | Understanding the Topic and Main Idea

A. Text. Answer the questions and write *MI* for *Main Idea*, *G* for *Too General*, and *S* for *Too Specific*. Discuss your answers with a partner.

1. What is the topic of the text? _____

2. What is the main idea of the text?

   a. _____ Dye had to consult the ancient Roman sources in order to learn how soldiers acted 2,400 years ago for the movie *Alexander*.

   b. _____ Dye prepared the actors for the movie *Alexander*.

   c. _____ A technical adviser creates realistic settings for movies.

3. Are your answers for the topic and the main idea the same as the ones you determined after you previewed the text, or are your answers different? Explain. _____

_____

B. Paragraphs. Write *T* for *Topic* or *MI* for *Main Idea*, *G* for *Too General*, and *S* for *Too Specific*. Discuss your answers with a partner.

1. What is the topic for ¶7?

    a. _____ preparing the army for the battle scenes

    b. _____ cooking food in the desert

    c. _____ working hard

2. What is the main idea for ¶7?

    a. _____ Everyone worked hard.

    b. _____ To prepare his army for the film's big battle scenes, Dye subjected the actors to three weeks of extremely hard workouts.

    c. _____ The actors had to cook their own food in the desert.

3. What is the topic for ¶10?

    a. _____ Val Kilmer's face

    b. _____ the importance of creating historically accurate details

    c. _____ Oliver Stone's insistence on historically accurate detailing

4. What is the main idea for ¶10?

    a. _____ Val Kilmer's face is made up to look exactly as the skull discovered in King Philip's grave would have looked in life.

    b. _____ It is important to create accurate details when making a film about a real historical figure.

    c. _____ Oliver Stone insisted that his departments create historically accurate detailing wherever possible.

READING SKILL Understanding Supporting Details

A **supporting detail** provides evidence, proves, or supports a main idea. Writers use details to develop their arguments. Supporting details can be **facts, opinions, examples, data**, or **statistics**.

Reread ¶2 on page 74.

The main idea is: Dye's specialty is assisting directors to create realistic war environments for movies.

The supporting details are:

    a. Dye used his own experience in *Platoon*.

    b. Dye used firsthand accounts and archival film footage to research for *Saving Private Ryan*.

    c. Dye used works of ancient Roman scholars to research for *Alexander*.

These details all show how Dye recreates a realistic environment for war movies.

6 | Understanding Supporting Details

Check (✔) the two supporting details. Discuss your answers with a partner.

1. What are the two supporting details for the main idea of ¶**7**?

   ☐ a. Dye set up tents in the Moroccan desert.

   ☐ b. The actors went through the conditioning of a Macedonian soldier.

   ☐ c. Macedonian fighting was hand-to-hand.

2. What are the two supporting details for the main idea of ¶**10**?

   ☐ a. Kilmer's face was made up to look like the skull of Philip's would have in life.

   ☐ b. Philip came back from the grave.

   ☐ c. The silver drinking cups were identical to real ones found in Philip's grave.

VOCABULARY STRATEGY Understanding Vocabulary in Context—
Collocations

Collocations are groups of words that frequently occur together and are often idiomatic. Sometimes they can be understood from the context of the sentence; other times, they need to be looked up in a dictionary that contains collocations (not all dictionaries include them).

Read the following sentences.

1. Alexander died at age 32 after leading his army across 22,000 miles *on foot*. (¶1)

   What does *on foot* mean? In this sentence, *on foot* means *by walking*. We can tell from the sentence that Alexander was leading his army on his feet (literally), but the idiomatic meaning of *on foot* is *by walking*. The collocation is always *on foot*, not *by foot* or *with foot*.

2. Dye claims that no one in *modern times* had ever tried it. (¶5)

   What does *modern times* mean? In this sentence, *modern times* means *the present*. *Modern times* literally might seem like it means *many modern times* in a plural sense, but the collocation *modern times* simply means *the present*. The collocation is always *modern times*, not *new times* or *modern years*.

   Note: Phrasal verbs (see page 49) are one kind of collocation.

7 | Understanding Vocabulary in Context—Collocations

Select the best meaning for each collocation according to the text.

1. on horseback (¶1)

   a. leading a horse   b. standing on a horse   c. riding a horse

2. firm handshake (¶3)

   a. nervous handshake   b. strong handshake   c. weak handshake

3. to find out (¶4)

   a. to discover   b. to look outside   c. to go outside

4. to test out (¶6)

   a. to stop something   b. to take an exam   c. to try or experiment

5. to realize [a person's] vision (¶6)

   a. to believe a vision   b. to make a vision a reality   c. to understand a vision

8 | Discussing the Issues

Answer the questions and discuss your answers with a partner.

1. Do you think it is important for moviemakers to represent history accurately in historical movies? Why or why not?

2. Do you think historical movies help the viewer understand history better? Why or why not?

3. Think of a historical movie you have seen. Was it well made? Why or why not?

Text 3 | Ancient Egypt: A Timeline

1 | Getting Started

Answer the questions and briefly discuss your answers with a partner.

1. Have you ever studied or visited Egypt?

2. Check (✔) all the words that you would expect to find in a text about ancient Egypt.

☐ a. horses ☐ d. Romans ☐ g. the Nile

☐ b. mummy ☐ e. pyramids ☐ h. streets

☐ c. pharaoh ☐ f. prince ☐ i. Peru

3. What are the Ancient Egyptians famous for?

> **GRAPHICS** Understanding Timelines
>
> **Timelines** show a sequence of chronological events over a specific period of time. They can be drawn horizontally—like the one below—or vertically, as on the next page. **Preview** timelines by reading the title, any subtitles, the first date and event, and the last date and event.

2 | Active Previewing

Preview the timeline on the next page and then answer the questions. Discuss your answers with a partner.

1. Approximately how many years does this timeline cover?

2. How many different periods are covered in the timeline?

3. What is the topic of this timeline?

3 | Understanding the Graphics

Write each period on the horizontal timeline according to the timeline on the next page.

3000 B.C.E.	2500 B.C.E.	2000 B.C.E.	1500 B.C.E.	1000 B.C.E.

Early Dynastic

THE HISTORY OF ANCIENT EGYPT

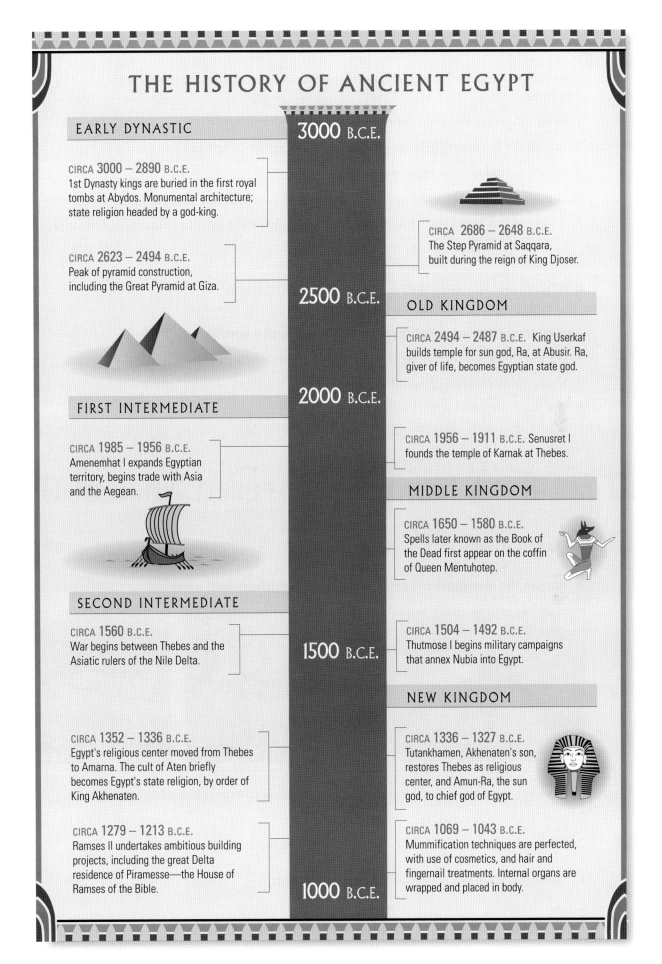

EARLY DYNASTIC

CIRCA **3000 – 2890** B.C.E.
1st Dynasty kings are buried in the first royal tombs at Abydos. Monumental architecture; state religion headed by a god-king.

CIRCA **2623 – 2494** B.C.E.
Peak of pyramid construction, including the Great Pyramid at Giza.

FIRST INTERMEDIATE

CIRCA **1985 – 1956** B.C.E.
Amenemhat I expands Egyptian territory, begins trade with Asia and the Aegean.

SECOND INTERMEDIATE

CIRCA **1560** B.C.E.
War begins between Thebes and the Asiatic rulers of the Nile Delta.

CIRCA **1352 – 1336** B.C.E.
Egypt's religious center moved from Thebes to Amarna. The cult of Aten briefly becomes Egypt's state religion, by order of King Akhenaten.

CIRCA **1279 – 1213** B.C.E.
Ramses II undertakes ambitious building projects, including the great Delta residence of Piramesse—the House of Ramses of the Bible.

3000 B.C.E.

CIRCA **2686 – 2648** B.C.E.
The Step Pyramid at Saqqara, built during the reign of King Djoser.

2500 B.C.E.

OLD KINGDOM

CIRCA **2494 – 2487** B.C.E. King Userkaf builds temple for sun god, Ra, at Abusir. Ra, giver of life, becomes Egyptian state god.

2000 B.C.E.

CIRCA **1956 – 1911** B.C.E. Senusret I founds the temple of Karnak at Thebes.

MIDDLE KINGDOM

CIRCA **1650 – 1580** B.C.E.
Spells later known as the Book of the Dead first appear on the coffin of Queen Mentuhotep.

CIRCA **1504 – 1492** B.C.E.
Thutmose I begins military campaigns that annex Nubia into Egypt.

1500 B.C.E.

NEW KINGDOM

CIRCA **1336 – 1327** B.C.E.
Tutankhamen, Akhenaten's son, restores Thebes as religious center, and Amun-Ra, the sun god, to chief god of Egypt.

CIRCA **1069 – 1043** B.C.E.
Mummification techniques are perfected, with use of cosmetics, and hair and fingernail treatments. Internal organs are wrapped and placed in body.

1000 B.C.E.

4 | Scanning

Scan the timeline for the answers to the questions. Discuss your answers with a partner.

1. In which period did Senusret I rule? _the First Intermediate period_

2. Where did Egypt's religious center move to during the New Kingdom period? _____

3. Which period was the most violent? _____

4. During which years were pyramids constructed? _____

5. What are two important changes that occurred in ancient Egypt's religious system, and when did they occur? _____

5 | Discussing the Issues

Answer the questions and discuss your answers with a partner.

1. Do you think it is important to know about developments in history? Why or why not?

2. How could timelines be useful?

3. Are there instances when timelines are not useful? Explain.

Text 4 | A Newly Discovered Ancient City

1 | Getting Started

A. Answer the questions and briefly discuss your answers with a partner.

1. Have you ever wanted to live in another time period to experience what it was like?

2. Look at the photos and try to identify what you see. Why do you think these sites might be famous?

3. What are two ancient historical sites that draw many tourists each year?

B. Check (✔) all of the countries that have pyramids.

☐ 1. Canada ☐ 3. France ☐ 5. Peru

☐ 2. Egypt ☐ 4. Mexico ☐ 6. Saudi Arabia

2 | Active Previewing

A. Preview the academic text below and tell a partner two things you remember about it.

B. Work as a class or in large groups. Try to name as many things as you can about the text.

C. Answer the questions with a partner.

1. What is the topic of this text?

2. What is the main idea of this text?

REMEMBER

Preview academic texts by reading the title, the subtitles, the first sentence of each paragraph, and the final sentence of the text. Preview longer academic texts a second time.
For more about *previewing academic texts*, see page 3.

3 | Reading and Recalling

A. Read the text. Stop after each paragraph and tell a partner two things that you remember about it.

First City in the New World?

Peru's Caral Suggests Civilization Emerged in the Americas 1,000 Years Earlier than Experts Believed

by John F. Ross

1 **Discovering a Lost Civilization**

Six earth-and-rock mounds rise out of the windswept desert of the Supe Valley near the coast of Peru. They appear to be natural hills in a desert region squeezed between the Pacific Ocean and the mountains of the Andean Cordillera. However, these are human-made pyramids, and compelling new evidence indicates they are the remains of a city that prospered nearly 5,000 years ago. If true, it would be the oldest city in the Americas and among the most ancient in all the world.

2 Research developed by Ruth Shady Solís, a Peruvian archaeologist at San Marcos University, suggests that Caral, as the huge complex of pyramids, plazas, and residential buildings is

known, was a thriving metropolis as Egypt's great pyramids were being built. The energetic archaeologist believes that Caral may also answer nagging questions[1] about the mysterious origins of the Inca, the civilization that once stretched from modern-day Ecuador to central Chile and created such cities as Cuzco and Machu Picchu. Caral may even hold a key to understanding the origins of civilizations everywhere.

3 **The Excavations Begin**

Though Caral was discovered in 1905, most archaeologists were uninterested in it because they believed the complex structures were fairly recent. But the huge scale of the pyramids had fascinated Shady since 1994, when she first came to the valley. She began excavations two years later. Fourteen miles from the coast and 120 miles north of Peru's capital city of Lima, Caral lies in a desert region that has no paved roads, electricity, or public water. Shady, who managed to get the help of 25 Peruvian soldiers for the excavations, often used her own money for the work.

4 For two months Shady and her crew searched for the broken remains of pots and containers, called potsherds, that most such sites contain. Not finding any only made her more excited; it

continued

---

[1] **nagging questions:** irritating or persistent questions

continued

meant Caral could be what archaeologists call pre-ceramic, or existing before pot-firing technology. Shady eventually concluded that Caral predated Olmec settlements to the north by 1,000 years. But colleagues remained skeptical. She needed proof.

5   In 1996, Shady's team began the mammoth task[2] of excavating Pirámide Mayor, the largest of the pyramids. After carefully clearing away several thousand years' worth of rubble and sand, they uncovered staircases, circular walls covered with remnants[3] of colored plaster, and squared brickwork. Finally, in the foundation, they found the preserved remains of reeds, or tall grasses, woven into bags known as shicras. The original workers, she guessed, must have filled these bags with stones from a quarry about a mile away and laid them atop one another inside retaining walls.

6   The Oldest Known City in the Americas

Shady knew that the reeds were ideal subjects for radiocarbon dating, a special technique used to determine the age of artifacts, and could prove her theory. In 1999, she sent samples of them to Jonathan Haas at Chicago's Field Museum and to Winifred Creamer at Northern Illinois University. In December 2000, Shady's suspicions were con-

firmed: the reeds were 4,600 years old. She took the news calmly, but Haas says he "was virtually in hysterics for three days afterward." In the April 27, 2001 issue of the journal *Science*, the three archaeologists reported that Caral and the other ruins of the Supe Valley are the central point of "some of the earliest population concentrations and corporate architecture in South America." The news surprised other scientists. "It was almost unbelievable," says Betty Meggers, an archaeologist at the Smithsonian Institution. "This data pushed back the oldest known dates for an urban center in the Americas by more than 1,000 years."

7   What amazed archaeologists was not just the age but the complexity and scope, or area, of Caral. Pirámide Mayor alone covers an area nearly the size of four football fields and is 60 feet tall. A 30-foot-wide staircase rises from a circular plaza at the foot of the pyramid, passing over three levels until it reaches the top of the platform. Here, there are the remains of an atrium, or an open place where people could gather, and a large fireplace. Thousands of manual laborers would have been needed to build such a huge project, as well as many architects, craftsmen, supervisors, and other managers. A ring of platform pyramids contains a large amphitheater, which could have held many hundreds of people during civic or religious events. Inside the amphitheater, Shady's team found 32 flutes made of the bones of seabirds. And, in April 2002, they uncovered 37 cornets made of animal bones. "Clearly, music played an important role in their society," says Shady.

8   Around the outer limits of Caral is a series of smaller mounds, various buildings, and residential complexes. Shady discovered a hierarchy[4] in living arrangements: large, well-kept rooms atop the pyramids for the rich and elite, ground-level complexes for craftsmen, and older and poorer homes far from the city center for workers.

9   Life in the Inland Desert

One important question was why Caral had been built in the first place. Even more important, why would people living comfortably in small communities near the Pacific Ocean with easy access to abundant marine food choose to move inland to a harsh desert? If she could answer this question, Shady believed she might begin to understand one of the most difficult questions in the field of anthro-

continued

---

[2] **mammoth task:** extremely large and complicated tasks

[3] **remnant:** small piece or part of something that is no longer whole

[4] **hierarchy:** a system of ranking or ordering

continued

pology today: What causes civilizations to arise? And what was it about the desert landscape of Peru's Supe Valley that caused a complex, hierarchical society to flourish there?

10   Her excavations convinced Shady that Caral had served as a major trade center for the region, ranging from the rain forests of the Amazon to the high forests of the Andes. She found fragments of the fruit of the achiote, a plant still used today in the rain forest as an aphrodisiac. And she found necklaces of snails and the seeds of the coca plant, neither of which came from Caral. This rich trading environment, Shady believes, allowed an elite group to develop that did not take part in the production of food. This group was able to become priests and planners, builders and designers. Thus, the class distinctions basic to an urban[5] society emerged.

11   But what sustained such a trading center and made travelers come there? Was it food? Shady and her team found the remains of fish, which must have come from the coast 14 miles to the west, in the excavations. But they also found evidence that the Caral people ate squash, sweet potatoes and beans. Shady theorized that Caral's early farmers redirected area rivers into trenches and canals, which still crisscross the Supe Valley today, to bring water to their fields. But because she found no traces of corn or other grains, which can be traded or stored and used to sustain a population in difficult times, she concluded that Caral's trade advantage was not based on storing large amounts of food supplies.

12   The Key to Caral's Existence

It was evidence of another crop in the excavations that gave Shady the best clue to the mystery of Caral's success. In nearly every excavated building, her team discovered great quantities of cottonseeds, fibers, and textiles. Her theory was proved when a large fishing net, discovered at an unrelated excavation on Peru's coast, turned out to be as old as Caral. "The farmers of Caral grew the cotton that the fishermen needed to make the nets," Shady speculates. "And the fishermen gave them shellfish and dried fish in exchange for these nets." In essence, the people of Caral enabled fishermen to work with larger and more effective nets, which made the resources of the sea more readily available.

13   Eventually, 17 other pyramid complexes arose around Caral across the 35-square-mile area of the Supe Valley. Then, around 1600 B.C.E., for reasons that may never be answered, the Caral civilization fell, though it didn't disappear overnight. "They had time to protect some of their architectural structures, burying them discreetly," says Shady. Other nearby areas, such as Chupacigarro, Lurihuasi and Miraya, became centers of power. But based on Caral's size and scope, Shady believes that it is indeed the mother city of the Incan civilization.

14   Shady plans to continue excavating Caral and says she would someday like to build a museum on the site. "So many questions still remain," she says. "Who were these people? How did they control the other populations?"

---

[5] **urban:** city

B. Read the text again without pausing. Tell your partner two new things that you remember.

C. Work as a class or in large groups. Try to name as many things as you can about the text.

4 | Understanding the Text

A. Answer as many questions as you can without looking at the text. Discuss your answers with a partner.

1. What is compelling about Caral? _____

2. Who is Ruth Shady Solís? _____

3. According to Shady, Caral might have been the mother city of which ancient civilization?

_____

_____

B. Complete the chart with the significance of each archaeological discovery according to the text. Discuss your answers with a partner.

Archaeological discovery of Caral	Significance
1. six earth and rock mounds in Caral	*actually man-made pyramids from a civilization nearly 5000 years old*
2. lack of potsherds	
3. shicras in the foundation of the Pyramide Major	
4. necklaces of snails, seeds of the coca plant	
5. cotton seeds, fibers, and textiles	

C. Number the statements in chronological order according to the text.

_____ a. For two months, Shady and her crew searched for potsherds.

_____ b. Shady would like to build a museum on the site of Caral.

___1___ c. Caral was first discovered in 1905.

_____ d. Shady's team found musical instruments (flutes and cornets) made of bird and animal bones.

_____ e. Shady's team began excavating the Pirámide Mayor.

5 | Understanding the Topic, Main Idea, and Supporting Details

A. Text. Answer the questions and write *MI* for *Main Idea*, *G* for *Too General*, and *S* for *Too Specific*. Discuss your answers with a partner.

1. What is the topic of the text? _____

2. What is the main idea of the text?

a. _____ Peru has many archaeological sites.

b. _____ Pot-firing technology is important for determining the age of a civilization or society.

    c. _____ An ancient city in Peru, called Caral, could be one of the oldest civilizations in the world.

3. Are your answers for the topic and the main idea the same as the ones you determined after you previewed the text, or are your answers different? Explain.

_____

B. Paragraphs. Write *T* for *Topic,* *MI* for *Main Idea,* and *SD* for *Supporting Detail.* Discuss your answers with a partner.

1. What are the topic, main idea, and supporting detail for ¶**1**?

    a. _____ An ancient city in Peru could be the oldest urban center in the Americas and among the oldest in the world.

    b. _____ an ancient city in the Supe Valley in Peru

    c. _____ Six earth and rock mounds in the Supe Valley are actually human-made pyramids.

2. What are the topic, main idea, and supporting detail for ¶**4**?

    a. _____ Not finding any potsherds made Shady excited.

    b. _____ The lack of potsherds led Shady to believe that Caral could be much older than other cultures in the area.

    c. _____ the lack of potsherds at Caral

3. What are the topic, main idea, and supporting detail for ¶**7**?

    a. _____ The complexity and scope of Caral is astonishing, and its construction was an enormous project.

    b. _____ the complexity and scope of Caral

    c. _____ The Pirámide Mayor is nearly the size of four football fields and is 60 feet tall.

4. What are the other supporting details for ¶**7**?

    The Pirámide Mayor is nearly as large as four football fields and is 60 feet tall.

_____

_____

_____

_____

6 | Understanding Possessive Adjectives

Answer the questions and discuss your answers with a partner.

1. In ¶**3**, what does *her* (her own money) refer to? _Shady_____

2. In ¶**4**, what does *her* (her crew) refer to? _____

3. In ¶**7**, what does *their* (their society) refer to? _____

4. In ¶**11**, what does *their* (their fields) refer to? _____

5. In ¶**13**, what does *their* (their architectural structures) refer to? _____

7 | Understanding Vocabulary in Context

A. Collocations. Select the best meaning for each collocation according to the text.

1. to hold a key to understanding (something) (¶2)

    a. to be an important clue to understanding something

    b. to open something that is locked

    c. to carry something to a new place

2. to remain skeptical (¶4)

    a. to change one's opinion

    b. to continue to doubt that something is true

    c. to stay behind someone or something

3. the outer limits (¶8)

    a. the border or edge of something

    b. the interior or inside of something

    c. the smallest part of something

B. Context Clues. Select the best meaning for each word or phrase according to the text.

1. remains (¶1)

    a. ancient ruins or buildings   b. natural hills   c. compelling evidence

2. thriving metropolis (¶2)

    a. the early pyramids   b. a building   c. a huge city

3. to conclude (¶4)

    a. to draw a map of the area   b. to refuse to believe   c. to decide after examining the facts

4. to predate (¶4)

    a. to come after   b. to come before   c. to happen at the same time

5. scope (¶7)

    a. beauty   b. area   c. remote location

8 | Discussing the Issues

Answer the questions and discuss your answers with a partner.

1. Do you think archaeology is a useful science? Why or why not?

2. What are three important things we can learn from Caral in regard to other civilizations?

3. Why might an archaeologist be willing to use his or her own money to fund research, such as Shady did with Caral?

Putting It On Paper

A. Write a five-paragraph essay on one of these topics.

1. Describe three ways in which archaeology, the study of ancient civilizations, can be useful or not useful.

2. Describe three ways in which movies about ancient civilizations or events can be harmful or not harmful.

Steps for your essay

a. In your first paragraph, clearly state your opinion about your topic and your general reason or reasons why.

b. Your second, third, and fourth paragraphs should each contain a separate idea that supports your opinion about your topic.

c. In your final paragraph, summarize the ideas you state in your essay.

B. Exchange essays with a partner. First, read your partner's essay and answer the questions in the checklist. Then give feedback to your partner.

> **NOTE**
>
> Each of your paragraphs should contain a main idea that is supported by details—facts, data, examples—that prove or illustrate your main idea. For more on *supporting details*, see page 77.

✔ CHECKLIST
1. Does ¶1 show your partner's opinion about the topic?
2. Do the three body paragraphs support the topic?
3. Does the final paragraph summarize the ideas contained in the essay?
4. Does each paragraph contain a main idea?
5. Do the details of each paragraph support the main idea?
6. Are you persuaded by your partner's reasons?
7. Is there any information in the essay that is not related to your partner's thesis? If so, please underline it on your partner's essay, and write it below:

_____

_____

_____

_____

_____

_____

_____

_____

C. Revise your work based on your partner's feedback.

Taking It Online | Pyramids

A. With a partner, use the Internet to research important pyramids found *outside* of Egypt and Peru.

1. Use Google (www.google.com) or another major search engine to begin your online research.

2. Search for websites with information about two pyramids in two different countries. (Try typing "pyramid" and the country name in the search field.)

3. Preview the websites.

ONLINE TIP

Use the *Advanced Search* feature on your search engine for more accurate search results.

B. Complete the tables with the information you find.

PYRAMID 1
Name:
Country:
Website address:
Who built this pyramid?
When was it built?
What was its purpose?
What is one interesting fact about this pyramid?

PYRAMID 2
Name:
Country:
Website address:
Who built this pyramid?
When was it built?
What was its purpose?
What is one interesting fact about this pyramid?

C. Following up. With your partner, choose one of your pyramids. Research the culture that built the pyramid and create a timeline for that culture.

Strange Phenomena

Answer the questions and briefly discuss your answers with a partner.

1. Do you believe that logic or science can explain everything in life?

2. Look at the photos and try to identify the phenomena. Do you believe in any of these phenomena?

3. Do you believe people who claim to have experienced any of the phenomena in the photos? Why or why not?

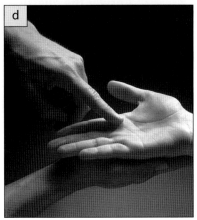

Text 1 | Psychic or Not?

1 | Getting Started

A. Check (✔) all of the activities that a psychic could claim to use his or her abilities for.

- [ ] **1.** cooking dinner
- [ ] **2.** finding missing people
- [ ] **3.** getting a job
- [ ] **4.** raising a family
- [ ] **5.** reading minds
- [ ] **6.** telling the future

B. Answer the questions and briefly discuss your answers with a partner.

1. Do you believe that some people have psychic abilities?

2. Would you ever visit a psychic?

3. Why do some people visit psychics?

2 | Active Previewing

A. Preview the magazine article on the next page and tell a partner two things you remember about it.

B. Work as a class or in large groups. Try to name as many things as you can about the text.

> **REMEMBER**
> Preview magazine articles by reading the title, the subtitles, the first sentence of each paragraph, and the final sentence of the text. For more about *previewing magazine articles,* see page 3.

C. Answer the questions with a partner.

1. What is the topic of this text?

2. What is the main idea of this text?

3 | Reading and Recalling

A. Read the text. Stop after each paragraph and tell a partner two things that you remember about it.

The Psychic Detective

BY BILL LAGATTUTA

1 Psychic Powers from a Young Age

Annette Martin says she's had unique psychic powers since the age of seven. One of her specialties is finding missing people, something she says she does by looking at a map of where they were last seen.

2   Martin says that all she requires is a victim's photograph: "I'm able to see what happened. I become the victim. I become the assailant[1]. And I also become the observer." In an effort to describe the psychic experience, Martin says that her "hand gets very hot" and that she can "feel" where the victim is going on a map.

3   Currently, Martin runs a successful business near San Francisco. But Martin's career as a psychic is her real claim to fame. Her paranormal perception has been a driving force[2] behind a multitude of police operations.

4 When Traditional Methods Failed

In 1997, Roberta Hauser approached Martin. Hauser was part of a search and rescue team in a state park near Pacifica, California, looking for a 71-year-old man who had disappeared from his home. A 40-person search team had already spent several days searching the area and had given up, but Hauser pressed on by herself for nine more weeks. "Pretty much every day after work I would come out here…and I would just slowly but surely cover sections of the map," Hauser continues. "[But] the probability of detection was very low."

5   As a last resort, a local police sergeant working on the case with Hauser contacted Martin and gave her a photograph and a map. "[I was] absolutely determined to find him," says Martin. "And I really felt like he was here. Well, my hand led me…over to where the area was. And I just followed the roads along, and I circled. He's in this area. That's where he is."

6   Hauser was skeptical, but she went out one final time with a search dog. It was then that the body was found in very deep shrubs[3]. "The mound is exactly in the center of the circle that she had drawn on the map," says Hauser. "She was absolutely right on the money."

7 Strong Believer in the Sheriff's Department

Martin has personally worked with more than a dozen police agencies over the years, she says. And in fact, one survey shows that 35 percent of urban police departments have used psychics at one time or another.

8   Rich Keaton is a retired detective with the Marin County Sheriff's Department that has relied on Martin's psychic insights in dozens of cases. He believes she has a gift, even though some people might be skeptical. "It's the unknown, and [people] can't explain it," he says. "[But] I would strongly put my belief, my integrity and my background in what Annette does and how she does it."

> "She started telling us specifics that only police officers knew," Keaton says.

9   Keaton has believed in Martin since he met her in 1975, when Martin had a vision of murder. "She started telling us specifics that only police officers knew," Keaton says.

10   Martin recalls: "I told them they would find [the suspect] about a year later, and they would find him wearing white…and that it was not going to be in California."

11   A year later, to the very week, the suspect was arrested in the state of Washington. "His occupation was that of a male nurse, or orderly in a hospital," Keaton recalls. "And he was wearing all white at the time that he was employed there." That made believers out of Keaton and some of his fellow officers.

12 What a Skeptic Says

But not Joe Nickell, who says he's been unimpressed by the whole experience. He's a columnist for the Skeptical Inquirer, a magazine that investigates claims of the paranormal. "She told us in this one case the guy was wearing white and he

continued

---

[1] **assailant:** attacker

[2] **driving force:** motivation, source of power

[3] **shrubs:** bushes, vegetation

continued

wouldn't be found in California. Was that all she told for several hours? Or were there lots of other things and those are being forgiven?" Nickell asks. "We call it retro-fitting[4]."

13   What about her finding that missing man in the park by drawing a small circle on the map? "What she did was very shrewdly ask all kinds of questions of that police officer, who helped her even further and told her all kinds of things," says Nickell. "It's probably perfectly sincere, not an act. But it's just the facility of a highly imaginative and emotional person and doesn't mean anything scientifically."

14   Nickell says there have been several controlled studies of psychics claiming to help police solve crimes: "When we do actual scientific studies, comparing psychics, with say, college students, the difference is the psychics tend to make more guesses, but they're no more successful."

15   Still, Martin says that her psychic visions are real, and Rich Keaton and Roberta Hauser remain impressed with her skills. For maybe, in the end, the extent of any psychic's powers is largely in the eye of the beholder[5].

[4] **retro-fitting:** modifying or fitting information to serve a purpose

[5] **to be in the eye of the beholder:** an expression meaning that people will have different opinions about something

B. Read the text again without pausing. Tell your partner two new things that you remember.

C. Work as a class or in large groups. Try to name as many things as you can about the text.

4 | Understanding the Text

A. Answer as many questions as you can without looking at the text. Discuss your answers with a partner.

1. How does Annette Martin help to find missing people and help to solve murder cases?

_____

2. What do the police think about Martin's abilities? _____

3. What does Joe Nickell think about Martin's apparent success at solving crimes?

_____

B. Check (✔) the correct answers according to the text. Discuss your answers with a partner.

Who said...?	Keaton	Nickell
1. Martin has a gift.	☐	☐
2. I remain unimpressed.	☐	☐
3. "She started telling us specifics that only police officers knew."	☐	☐
4. "It's just the facility of a highly imaginative person… and doesn't mean anything…"	☐	☐
5. Compared to college students, "psychics make more guesses, but they're no more successful."	☐	☐

5 | Understanding the Topic, Main Idea, and Supporting Details

A. Text. Answer the questions and discuss your answers with a partner.

1. What is the topic of the text? _____

2. What is the main idea of the text? _____

_____

_____

3. Are your answers for the topic and the main idea the same as the ones you determined after you previewed the text, or are your answers different? _____

B. Paragraphs. Write the topic for each paragraph, and then write *MI* for *Main Idea* and *SD* for *Supporting Detail* on the blanks. Discuss your answers with a partner.

1. What is the topic of ¶1? _____

a. _____ To find missing people, Annette Martin looks at a map of where they were last seen.

b. _____ Annette Martin uses her psychic powers to help police find missing people.

2. What is the topic of ¶2? _____

a. _____ Martin can see what happens.

b. _____ Martin sees herself as the assailant.

3. What is the topic of ¶11? _____

a. _____ The suspect was arrested a year later in the state of Washington.

b. _____ The suspect was a male nurse.

6 | Understanding Vocabulary in Context—Idioms

Select the best meaning for each idiom according to the text.

1. claim to fame (¶3)

   a. something not true   b. an everyday job   c. the reason someone is famous

2. slowly but surely (¶4)

   a. carelessly   b. carefully   c. helplessly

3. as a last resort (¶5)

   a. as a final attempt   b. as a first option   c. at the best hotel

4. right on the money (¶6)

   a. correct   b. incorrect   c. rich

5. at one time or another (¶7)

   a. always   b. never   c. at least once

A **fact** is something that is true about a subject and can be tested or proven.

Read the following sentence.

In 1997, Roberta Hauser approached Martin. (¶4)

This statement is a fact because it can be proven through documentation.

An **opinion** is what someone thinks about a subject. Opinions may be based on facts, but they show a person's feelings about something and cannot be tested or proven.

Read the following sentence.

Currently, Martin runs a successful business near San Francisco. (¶3)

The word *successful* cannot be tested or proven. It can be tested or proven that Martin runs a business near San Francisco, but the success of his business cannot be measured objectively. It is only the writer's opinion that Martin's business is successful. Someone else might not agree that Martin has a successful business.

7 | Reading Critically—Fact and Opinion

Write F for *Fact* or O for *Opinion*. Discuss your answers with a partner.

_____ 1. Martin's career as a psychic is her real claim to fame. (¶3)

_____ 2. Annette Martin has a gift. (¶8)

_____ 3. Keaton met Martin in 1975. (¶9)

_____ 4. A year after Martin first talked with police in 1975, the suspect was arrested in the state of Washington. (¶11)

_____ 5. Martin's work is probably perfectly sincere, not an act. (¶13)

8 | Discussing the Issues

Answer the questions and discuss your answers with a partner.

1. Martin claims she uses her psychic abilities to solve crimes. Nickell is skeptical. Whom do you find more convincing? Why?

2. If you were missing something or someone, and a person claiming to be psychic offered to help you find that thing or person, would you accept? Why or why not?

3. According to the article, 35 percent of urban police departments have used psychics in order to help them solve crimes. What do you think about this?

Text 2 | New York Taste

1 | Getting Started

A. Answer the questions and briefly discuss your answers with a partner.

1. Do you enjoy music?

2. Which of the five senses do you use when you listen to music?

3. How does listening to music affect you?

4. Check (✔) whether you agree or disagree. Briefly discuss your answers with a partner.

I think that...	Agree	Disagree
1. ...it is possible to taste words.	☐	☐
2. ...each letter of the alphabet has a special color.	☐	☐
3. ...music can be experienced physically.	☐	☐
4. ...it is possible to see music.	☐	☐
5. ...sounds have colors.	☐	☐

2 | Active Previewing

A. Preview the newspaper article on the next page by reading the first three paragraphs. Then answer these questions with a partner.

1. Who (what group of people) is the main subject of this article?

2. What do these people experience?

3. Where in the body does this condition come from?

4. When was this condition discovered?

B. Work as a class or in large groups. Try to name as many things as you can about the text.

C. Then answer these questions with a partner.

1. What is the topic of this text?

2. What is the main idea of this text?

> **REMEMBER**
>
> Preview newspaper articles by reading the title and any captions, looking at any photos, and reading the first two to four paragraphs.
> For more on *previewing newspaper articles*, see page 28.

3 | Reading and Recalling

A. Read the text. Stop after each paragraph and tell a partner two things that you remember about it.

A Sixth Sense

BY VICKI MABREY

1 **Ordinary People**

This is a story about ordinary people who see and feel things the rest of us don't. They have a rare brain condition called synesthesia, in which some of the senses—normally quite distinct—are joined together, creating almost literally a sixth sense. Music is not only heard, it's seen and felt; words can have flavors, and flavors can have color.

2 Here's what four synesthetes experience:

3 Ray McAllister sees music: "A bright flash of lavender getting dimmer and dimmer; now we're going over a pink staircase, some lavender violins."

4 Carol Crane feels music: "I always feel guitars on my ankles and violins on my face."

5 For Carol Steen, every letter has a color: "Z is the color of beer, a light ale."

6 And James Wannerton tastes words: for him "New York" tastes like "runny eggs." "London is mashed potato, but it's extremely lumpy mashed potatoes."

7 These people are not on drugs, and they don't have any brain disease. They haven't had a stroke. This is an innate condition, not an acquired one.

8 **Medically Speaking**

Neurologist Richard Cytowic explored this surreal[1] world of synesthesia in his book, *The Man Who Tasted Shapes*. He's documented[2] hundreds of cases of synesthesia. "You know the word anesthesia, which means no sensation[3]," explains Cytowic. "Synesthesia means joined sensation, and some people are born with two or more of their senses hooked together so that my voice, for example, is not just something that they hear, but it's also something that they might see or taste or feel." He says it's a condition that has been known to medicine and psychology for 300 years.

9 **Isolation**

While most people simply hear a concert, Carol Crane actually feels it—every instrument, every note. She says it's very pleasant, for the most part, but that when she leaves a symphony, for example, instead of feeling energized, she feels as if she's "just drained."

10 For New York artist Carol Steen, synesthesia is inspiration. She translates music into art, but she says all sounds produce color for her.

11 Though there are dozens of forms of synesthesia, Carol Steen has the most common: seeing letters and numbers in color. The colors never change. She's seen the same letters in the same colors her whole life. But Carol Crane sees those letters in different colors.

12 Synesthetes may disagree on what color the letter "A" is, but there's one thing they concur on. Instead of feeling like they belong with the rest of the world, synesthetes feel isolated. Many are embarrassed, afraid of being ridiculed[4], so often they keep their condition to themselves.

13 "I remember over the years," says Crane, "having discrete experiences with people such as asking them, 'What color is your three or five' or something like that, and I would get a look like 'Are you crazy?' So I stopped asking the question."

14 About four years ago, Crane was relieved to discover that she was, in fact, normal, even though her condition was abnormal. She found there was a name for it and that there were other people who had the same experiences. She also discovered that people close to her were keeping the same secret. Her sister, niece, and son all have synesthesia; it runs in families.

15 **Inside the Brain**

Although most people have never heard of synesthesia, it is hardly a new discovery. By 1910, scientists had written dozens of papers describing the condition. It was a curiosity, believed to affect creative types—the writer Vladimir Nabokov had it, and so does the painter David Hockney.

16 Medical technology can now reveal what happens inside the synesthete's mind. Dr. Vilyanur Ramachandran, a neurologist who studies quirks, or

continued

---

[1] **surreal:** having a strange, dreamlike quality

[2] **to document:** to write down and support with proof—facts, examples, and other data

[3] **sensation:** a perception or awareness connected with one of the senses

[4] **to ridicule:** to make fun of

continued

oddities, of the brain, was able to image the brain of 27-year-old McAllister, the man who sees music.

17   During the brain scan, music stimulated McAllister's audio cortex—and his visual cortex. "That area lit up in him," says Ramachandran. "So you know there was activity in the visual area of his brain even though he was only listening to music."

18   McAllister describes listening to music as a *Fantasia*-like experience: "Explosions of color all over the place. It looks very beautiful." This is all the more surprising since McAllister is blind. He lost his sight when he was 12, the result of a degenerative[5] eye disease. But he never lost his synesthesia.

19   **What Causes Synesthesia**
    Though scientists can prove synesthesia exists, they still don't know what causes it. Some think it's cross-wiring in the brain; others believe we're all born with synesthesia, but our senses separate as we grow older.

20   Researchers like Cytowic aren't looking for a cure for synesthesia; they're studying synesthetes for the remarkable clues it offers to the mysteries of the human mind. "These people experience the world in a different way," he says. "Their senses are wired together differently."

21   Crane wouldn't have it wired any other way. "I just think the world would be rather flat," she says.

---

[5] **degenerative:** said of a condition that progressively weakens and destroys the functioning of an organ or tissue

B. Read the text again without pausing. Tell your partner two new things that you remember.

C. Work as a class or in large groups. Try to name as many things as you can about the text.

4 | Understanding the Text

A. Answer as many questions as you can without looking at the text. Discuss your answers with a partner.

1. Briefly, what is synesthesia? _____

_____

2. What are some examples of synesthesia? _____

_____

3. Is all synesthesia a new medical discovery? _____

B. Check (✔) the statements that are true according to the text.

With synesthesia...
☐   1. ...music can be felt.
☐   2. ...painting can be danced.
☐   3. ...words can be tasted.
☐   4. ...music can be seen.
☐   5. ...letters are all one color.

5 | Understanding the Topic, Main Idea, and Supporting Details

A. **Text.** Answer the questions and discuss your answers with a partner.

1. What is the topic of the text? _____

_____

2. What is the main idea of the text? _____

_____

_____

3. Are your answers for the topic and the main idea the same as the ones you determined after you previewed the text, or are your answers different? _____

B. **Paragraphs.** Answer the questions and write *MI* for *Main Idea*. Discuss your answers with a partner.

1. What is the topic of ¶1? _____

2. What is the main idea of ¶1?

   a. _____ The senses are normally quite distinct.

   b. _____ With a rare brain condition called synesthesia, flavors have color.

   c. _____ Synesthesia is a rare brain condition in which some of the senses are joined together.

3. What are the supporting details for ¶1? _Music is seen and felt._____

_____

4. What is the topic of ¶2? _____

5. What is the main idea of ¶2?

   a. _____ Synesthetes feel isolated because of their condition.

   b. _____ Synesthetes disagree about what color the letter "A" is.

   c. _____ Synesthetes do not belong with the rest of the world.

6. What are the supporting details for ¶2? _Many are embarrassed._____

_____

7. What is the topic of ¶7?

_____

8. What is the main idea of ¶7?

   a. _____ During the brain scan, McAllister's visual cortex lit up while he was listening to music.

   b. _____ Music stimulates McAllister's visual cortex.

   c. _____ Dr. Ramachandran gave McAllister a brain scan.

9. What is the supporting detail for ¶7?

_____

_____

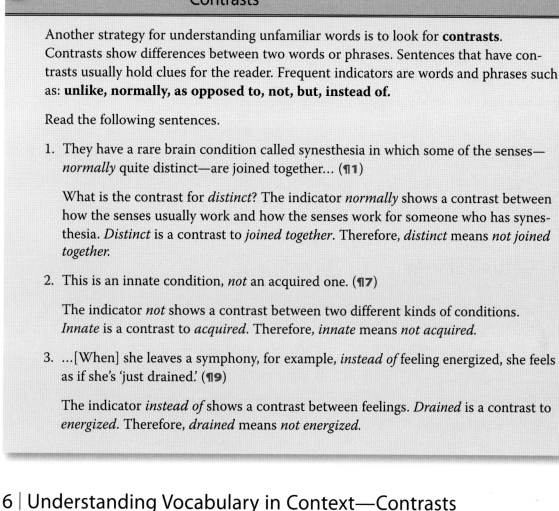

VOCABULARY STRATEGY Understanding Vocabulary in Context—
Contrasts

Another strategy for understanding unfamiliar words is to look for **contrasts**. Contrasts show differences between two words or phrases. Sentences that have contrasts usually hold clues for the reader. Frequent indicators are words and phrases such as: **unlike, normally, as opposed to, not, but, instead of.**

Read the following sentences.

1. They have a rare brain condition called synesthesia in which some of the senses—*normally* quite distinct—are joined together... (¶1)

   What is the contrast for *distinct*? The indicator *normally* shows a contrast between how the senses usually work and how the senses work for someone who has synesthesia. *Distinct* is a contrast to *joined together*. Therefore, *distinct* means *not joined together.*

2. This is an innate condition, *not* an acquired one. (¶7)

   The indicator *not* shows a contrast between two different kinds of conditions. *Innate* is a contrast to *acquired*. Therefore, *innate* means *not acquired.*

3. ...[When] she leaves a symphony, for example, *instead of* feeling energized, she feels as if she's 'just drained.' (¶9)

   The indicator *instead of* shows a contrast between feelings. *Drained* is a contrast to *energized*. Therefore, *drained* means *not energized.*

6 | Understanding Vocabulary in Context—Contrasts

Write the contrast for each word according to the text.

1. to concur (on) (¶12) _____

2. isolated (¶12) _____

3. abnormal (¶14) _____

7 | Reading Critically—Fact and Opinion

Write *F* for *Fact* or *O* for *Opinion*. Discuss your answers with a partner.

___O___ **1.** Neurologist Richard Cytowic has documented hundreds of cases of synesthesia. (¶8)

_____ **2.** Synesthesia is inspiration. (¶10)

_____ **3.** There are dozens of forms of synesthesia. (¶11)

_____ **4.** We are all born with synesthesia, and then the senses separate as we grow older. (¶19)

_____ **5.** I just think the world would be rather flat [without synethesia]. (¶21)

8 | Discussing the Issues

Answer the questions and discuss your answers with a partner.

1. In your opinion, which person had the most unusual form of synesthesia? Why?

2. In Carol Crane's opinion, "the world would be rather flat" without synesthesia. Do you think it would be interesting or difficult to have this condition? Why or why not?

3. The writer describes synesthesia as being "almost literally a sixth sense." Do you agree? Why or why not?

Text 3 | Believe It or Not

1 | Getting Started

A. Match each word or phrase on the left with the best definition on the right. Briefly discuss your answers with a partner.

_____ 1. extraterrestrials (ETs)

_____ 2. ghosts

_____ 3. astrology

_____ 4. extrasensory perception (ESP)

_____ 5. haunted houses

a. spirits of dead people

b. houses with spirits of dead people

c. aliens; beings from other planets

d. the study of stars and planets, as related to the lives of human beings

e. the ability to receive information without using any of the normal five senses (using a sixth sense)

B. Answer the question and discuss your answer with a partner

Which of the above phenomena, if any, do you believe in?

2 | Active Previewing

Preview the bar graph below and then answer the questions with a partner.

1. What is the title of the bar graph?

2. Which years are included in the bar graph?

3. What is the topic of this bar graph?

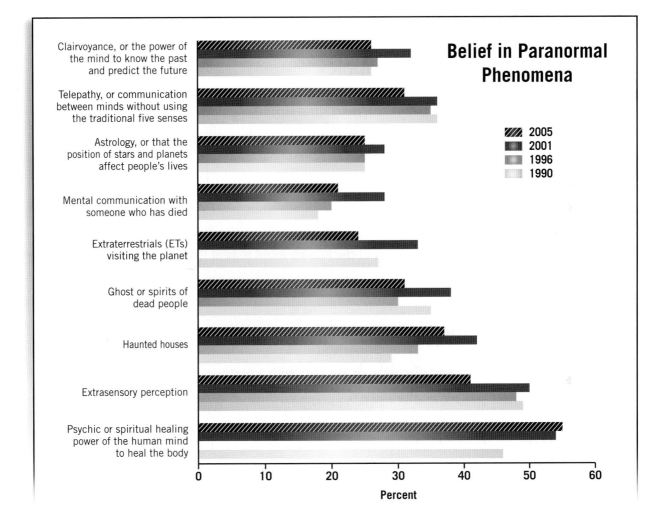

3 | Scanning

Scan the bar graph for the answers to the questions. Discuss your answers with a partner.

1. Which year showed the most believers in extrasensory perception? _____

2. Which paranormal activity had the most believers in 2005? _____

3. Which paranormal activity had the most believers in 1990? _____

4. Which paranormal activity showed an increase in believers between 2001 and 2005?

    _____

5. What percentage of people believed in ghosts in 1996? _____

4 | Understanding the Graphics

According to the bar graph, rank the years from largest number of believers to smallest number of believers.

1. Mental communication with someone who has died: _2001, 2005, 1996, 1990_____

2. Extraterrestrials visiting the planet: _____

3. Haunted houses: _____

4. Extrasensory perception (ESP): _____

5. Psychic or spiritual healing power of the human mind to heal the human body: _____

    _____

5 | Discussing the Issues

Answer the questions and discuss your answers with a partner.

1. Do you find any of the results in the bar graph surprising? Why or why not?

2. Which of the paranormal activities mentioned in the bar graph, if any, would be the most believed in your family? Why?

3. Survey your classmates on their beliefs of the paranormal and create a bar graph that shows the results. How do your classmates' beliefs compare with the results in the bar graph on page 103?

Text 4 | Coincidence or Random Chance

1 | Getting Started

A. Check (✔) all of the events that have happened to you. Briefly discuss your answers with a partner.

- [ ] 1. dreaming something that later comes true
- [ ] 2. meeting a stranger and discovering that you share the same birthday
- [ ] 3. thinking about someone and then getting a phone call from that person minutes or seconds later
- [ ] 4. meeting someone you know in a place neither of you has been to before
- [ ] 5. saying exactly the same thing at the same time as someone else

B. Answer the questions and briefly discuss your answers with a partner.

1. Do you think coincidences are important or that they simply happen by chance?

2. What is one example of coincidence being connected to scientific progress?

3. Why do you think some people believe that coincidences happen for important reasons?

> **REMEMBER**
>
> Preview academic texts by reading the title, the subtitles, the first sentence of each paragraph, and the final sentence of the text. Preview longer academic texts a second time.
>
> For more about *previewing academic texts,* see page 3.

2 | Active Previewing

A. Preview the academic text on the next page and tell a partner two things you remember about it.

B. Work as a class or in large groups. Try to name as many things as you can about the text.

C. Answer the questions with a partner.

1. What is the topic of this text?
2. What is the main idea of this text?

3 | Reading and Recalling

A. Read the text. Stop after each paragraph and tell a partner two things that you remember about it.

The Power of Coincidence

by Jill Neimark

1 Lucky Accidents

One thing is certain about coincidence: the phenomenon fascinates believers and skeptics alike. Coincidence allows us to examine one of the most basic questions we can ask: are the events of our lives objective or subjective? Is there an overall purpose to the universe, or are we the lucky accidents of evolution? Is there an underlying order, or is it we who give meaning to a basically meaningless world?

2 For skeptics, a coincidence is chance; it simply obeys the laws of probability and has no special meaning. John Allen Paulos, professor of mathematics at Temple University in Philadelphia, feels that the most "incredible coincidence imaginable would be the complete absence of all coincidence."

3 For believers, however, coincidence is the purposeful occurrence of two seemingly unrelated events. Paulos feels that people who believe in coincidences have a need to give greater importance to their lives than they really have. He believes that people who believe in coincidence find it depressing to hear someone say, "It just happened, and it doesn't mean anything."

4 The argument is not likely to be resolved any time soon. Anomalies—facts or events that are unrelated or difficult to classify—can be confusing and controversial. Lately, though, the phenomenon of coincidence has begun to yield new scientific insights. Humans may have an innate[1] ability to connect anomalies in a meaningful way. Many brain functions—including our ability to learn the meaning of words or understand unspoken social laws—depend on our natural ability to notice coincidences. Mathematicians, cognitive scientists, and paranormal researchers have begun studying the problem of coincidence in a different way—by applying statistics and probability. Are coincidences easily explained, or are they so improbable they must signify something?

5 Comets, Dogs, and Coincidence

As an example, people long believed comets to be cosmic[2] messages of some kind: the Romans recorded that a comet appeared when Julius Caesar was assassinated[3] in 44 B.C.E. In England in 1066, a comet appeared just before the Battle of Hastings was fought over the throne, and another before the Great Plague—a disease that killed around 100,000 people in 1665. According to the lore of the Incan Indians in South America, a comet appeared just before the arrival of Francisco Pizarro, who arrived in 1532 to conquer[4] them. Were comets really signs of coming disaster, or were these just strange coincidences?

6 In 1705 English astronomer Edmund Halley was looking through old records of comets when he noticed a coincidence: the bright comets of 1531, 1607, and 1682 had almost the same orbits and appeared approximately every 75 years. Halley concluded they were one comet and predicted it would reappear in 1758. On Christmas night of 1758, Halley's Comet appeared, forever changing our understanding of comets.

7 Indeed, coincidences can actually help science progress. Josh Tenenbaum, a cognitive scientist at MIT, sees this as an interesting contradiction. "On the one hand they seem to be the source of our greatest irrationalities—seeing connections when science tells us they aren't there. On the other hand, some of our greatest feats of scientific discovery depend on coincidences."

8 According to Tenenbaum, many of the connections our minds make revolve around coincidence. One of our brains' functions is to notice anomalies and to use them in order to learn more. Since coincidence operates at such a basic level in our brains, it is not surprising that we sometimes see connections where they do not exist. But do we fall into that trap too often?

continued

---

[1] **innate:** existing in; belonging to; part of

[2] **cosmic:** from the universe, or from a greater power in the universe

[3] **assassinate:** to murder (usually used in reference to a political person)

[4] **conquer:** to defeat, usually by use of force

9 It's Just a Coincidence!

When he began writing his best-selling book of strange coincidences, *When God Winks*, SQuire Rushnell was wondering about former U.S. presidents John Adams and Thomas Jefferson, two men who shaped the Declaration of Independence of the United States of America. It is a famous coincidence that both men died exactly 50 years after the signing of that document—July 4, 1826.

10 "I sat in my small study wondering whether there were more coincidences connecting the two men," recalls Rushnell. He pulled a reference book off his shelf, but it had no useful information. "Then I noticed a thin old volume right next to the reference book. I'd brought it back in a box of books after my grandfather's funeral and never noticed it before." The book was a collection of speeches, and the first one was a speech written after the deaths of Adams and Jefferson. The speech described many coincidences linking the two men. In later research, Rushnell discovered that the book was available in only one public library in the Eastern U.S., the rare book section of the Library of Congress. "Yet here was a copy from my grandfather, sitting right there on my shelf, just when I needed it," exclaims Rushnell.

11 According to the mathematicians who study the laws of probability, the coincidence was not as unlikely as one might believe. "In ten years there are 5 million minutes," says Irving Jack Good, a professor in the department of statistics at Virginia Polytechnic Institute in Blacksburg. "That means each person has plenty of opportunity to have some remarkable coincidences in his life."

12 Improbable occurrences are to be expected, say statisticians, especially considering there are 6.5 billion people on the planet. "The information-rich environment of modern life itself is a source of many coincidences," says John Paulos. He says even dreams that come true can be explained by probability. Americans, for example, dream approximately 600 million hours each night (300 million people dreaming two hours a night). According to the laws of probability, say statisticians, some of those dreams must be identical to real events.

13 The Other Side of Probability

We may be highly skilled at detecting and connecting anomalous events, but that doesn't help us understand events so impressive that they are readily noticed—but not easily explained. Dean Radin is senior scientist at the Institute of Noetic Sciences in Petaluma, California—an institute that studies psychic phenomena—and author of *The Conscious Universe: The Scientific Truth of Psychic Phenomena*. He says he has no argument with scientists who believe it is the laws of probability that govern coincidence but that he just doesn't "accept that this explanation is correct 100 percent of the time."

14 In laboratory studies, for example, Radin has found that people seem to know when they are going to observe disturbing photographs. A measurement of electrical activity on their skin rises before they view disturbing photos that are not purposely, but randomly selected by a computer. The same changes do not occur before neutral or calming photos appear.

15 Radin has been testing coincidence on a global scale since 1998. He is specifically interested in studying whether events that have a worldwide impact are able to focus people's consciousness, or awareness, and whether that consciousness can influence the functioning of machines. In order to study this, 75 researchers around the world have volunteered to join the Global Consciousness Project, which is directed by Radin and psychologist Roger Nelson of Princeton University. There are 75 machines, called "random number generators," that are monitored by the researchers. The machines produce numbers based on electronic noise, such as the static one hears when changing radio stations. The goal is to measure whether events that focus mass consciousness (the minds of everyone on the planet) are able to affect the machines.

16 The project has studied 168 significant events that occurred over a five-year period. On September 11, 2001, a few hours before the World Trade Center was attacked, there was a large, anomalous spike, or sharp increase, in the 37 generators being monitored at that time. In a sense, the generators were extremely "noisy," says Radin. "Over the course of the rest of the

continued

continued

day, the opposite happened. There was a drop in magnitude that was uncharacteristically quiet and unique for that entire year." On March 11, 2004, after the attacks in Madrid, it was also unusually "noisy." The next day, however, during the demonstrations in Spain, there was once again uncharacteristic coherence, or "quiet," from the machines. Radin hypothesizes[5] that disasters upset global consciousness, while mass demonstrations and celebrations lead to a coherent mind field, which shifts these supposedly random machines toward "quiet."

17   What do these findings have to do with coincidence? Computer scientist Richard Shoup is president of the Boundary Institute in Saratoga, California, another institute that studies psychic phenomena. He believes this kind of data may challenge the assumption, or current accepted theory, of fundamental randomness that is at the heart of much scientific thought today. If so, it will also challenge the worldview of people who believe coincidence is just chance.

---

[5] **hypothesize:** to make an educated guess

B. Read the text again without pausing. Tell your partner two new things that you remember.

C. Work as a class or in large groups. Try to name as many things as you can about the text.

4 | Understanding the Text

A. Answer as many questions as you can without looking at the text. Discuss your answers with a partner.

1. What do skeptics think coincidence is? _____

_____

2. What do believers think coincidence represents? _____

_____

3. What did people used to believe about comets? _____

_____

4. What do many mathematicians believe about coincidence? _____

_____

5. Based on his work with "random number generators," what is Dean Radin's theory?

_____

_____

B. Check (✔) *True* or *False* according to the text. If the statement is false, correct it. Discuss your answers with a partner.

Statements	True	False
1. For skeptics, coincidence has special meaning. _____ _____	☐	☐
2. Edmond Halley concluded that the bright comets of 1531, 1607, and 1682 were in fact just two comets. _____ _____	☐	☐
3. According to Josh Tenenbaum, some of our greatest feats of scientific discovery depend on coincidence. _____ _____	☐	☐
4. SQuire Rushnell discovered a book on John Adams and Thomas Jefferson in his own bookshelves that was available in only one public library in the Eastern U.S., the Library of Congress. _____ _____	☐	☐
5. The day after the attacks in Madrid, the random noise generators were unusually noisy. _____ _____	☐	☐

5 | Understanding the Topic, Main Idea, and Supporting Details

A. Text. Answer the questions and write *MI* for *Main Idea*. Discuss your answers with a partner.

1. What is the topic of the text? _____

2. What is the main idea of the text?

   a. _____ Skeptics and believers alike think that coincidence is a fascinating subject that allows us to ask important questions about the nature of the universe.

   b. _____ Believers think that coincidence is the purposeful occurrence of two seemingly unrelated events.

   c. _____ Coincidence is not as unlikely as one might believe.

3. Are your answers for the topic and the main idea the same as the ones you determined after you previewed the text, or are your answers different? _____

B. Paragraphs. Answer the questions and write *MI* for *Main Idea*. Discuss your answers with a partner.

1. What is the topic of ¶5? _____

2. What is the main idea of ¶5?

   a. _____ Comets used to be signs of coming disaster.

   b. _____ For a long time, people believed that comets were cosmic messages.

   c. _____ A comet appeared before Francisco Pizarro arrived to conquer the Incan Indians.

3. What are the supporting details for ¶5? <u>*A comet appeared when Julius Caesar*</u>
   <u>*was assassinated.*</u>
   _____
   _____

4. What is the topic of ¶11? _____

5. What is the main idea of ¶11?

   a. _____ Mathematicians are studying probability.

   b. _____ According to mathematicians, coincidence is more likely than one might believe.

   c. _____ Each person has plenty of opportunity to have some remarkable coincidences in life.

6. What are the supporting details for ¶11? *In ten years there are 5 million* *minutes.* _____

_____

_____

7. What is the topic of ¶16? _____

8. What is the main idea of ¶16?

   a. _____ After studying 168 significant events over a five-year period, Radin believes that these kinds of events lead to shifts in global consciousness.

   b. _____ On March 11, 2004, the random noise generators were unusually noisy.

   c. _____ Radin's project has studied many significant events over a number of years.

9. What are the supporting details for ¶16? _____

_____

_____

_____

6 | Understanding Vocabulary in Context—Synonyms

Write the synonym for each word or phrase according to the text.

1. the Great Plague (¶5) *a disease that killed around 100,000 in 1665* _____

2. consciousness (¶15) _____

3. mass consciousness (¶15) _____

4. spike (¶16) _____

5. assumption (¶17) _____

7 | Reading Critically—Fact and Opinion

Write *F* for *Fact* or *O* for *Opinion*. Discuss your answers with a partner.

__F__ 1. Coincidence fascinates believers and skeptics alike. (¶1)

_____ 2. The argument between believers and skeptics is not likely to be resolved any time soon. (¶4)

_____ 3. Considering there are 6.5 billion people on the planet, improbable occurrences are to be expected. (¶12)

_____ 4. In laboratory studies, a measurement of electrical activity on people's skin rises before they view upsetting photographs that are randomly selected by a computer. (¶14)

_____ 5. Radin has been testing coincidence on a global scale since 1998. (¶15)

B. With a partner, find two new facts and two new opinions in the text. Write the number of the paragraph where you find the information. Discuss your answers with a partner.

Fact 1: (¶_____) _____

Fact 2: (¶_____) _____

Opinion 1: (¶_____) _____

Opinion 2: (¶_____) _____

8 | Discussing the Issues

Answer the questions and discuss your answers with a partner.

1. Which theory do you believe: that coincidences are just random chance or that coincidences are occurrences that have a deeper meaning to them? Why?

2. Why do you think that people, prior to Edmund Halley's discovery, would have believed that comets foretold disaster?

3. According to the data recorded by the random number generators, people's minds can affect machines. What is your opinion about Dean Radin's hypothesis that people's thoughts can affect the world?

Putting It On Paper

A. Write a five-paragraph essay on one of these topics.

1. Describe three reasons why you believe psychic ability is or is not real.

2. Describe three reasons why you believe coincidence either does or does not have a deeper meaning than random chance.

Steps for your essay

    a. In your first paragraph, clearly state your opinion about your topic and your general reason or reasons why.

    b. Your second, third, and fourth paragraphs should each contain a separate reason that supports your opinion about your topic.

    c. In your final paragraph, summarize the ideas you state in your essay.

> **NOTE**
>
> Each of your paragraphs should contain a main idea that is supported by details—facts, data, examples—that prove or illustrate your main idea. For more on *supporting details*, see page 77.

B. Exchange essays with a partner. First, read your partner's essay and answer the questions in the checklist. Then give feedback to your partner.

✓ CHECKLIST
1. Does ¶1 show your partner's opinion about the topic?
2. Do the three body paragraphs support the topic?
3. Does the final paragraph summarize the ideas contained in the essay?
4. Does each paragraph contain a main idea?
5. Do the details of each paragraph support the main idea?
6. Are you persuaded by your partner's reasons?
7. Is there any information in the essay that is not related to your partner's thesis? If so, please underline it on your partner's essay, and write it below:

_____

_____

_____

_____

_____

_____

_____

_____

B. Revise your work based on your partner's feedback.

Taking It Online | Coincidences

A. With a partner, use the Internet to research unusual coincidences.

1. Use Google (www.google.com) or another major search engine to begin your online research.

2. Search for websites with information about three unusual coincidences. (Try typing "amazing," "unusual," or "interesting," and "coincidence" in the search field.)

3. Preview the websites.

ONLINE TIP

On the search results page, click on the word <u>Cached</u> that follows the listing for the website you want. The website will open with your search terms highlighted.

B. Complete the table with the information you find.

Coincidence 1
Name:
Website address:
Summary of coincidence:

Coincidence 2
Name:
Website address:
Summary of coincidence:

Coincidence 3
Name:
Website address:
Summary of coincidence:

C. **Following up.** Choose one of the coincidences you researched and discuss it with the class or in small groups. Can you think of any explanation(s) for why that coincidence may have occurred?

Chapter 6 Rethinking Business

Answer the questions and briefly discuss your answers with a partner.

1. Do you believe that businesses are an important part of a community?

2. Look at the photos and try to identify the business activities.

3. What is your opinion about these kinds of businesses?

Text 1 | The Future of Business

1 | Getting Started

A. Answer the questions and briefly discuss your answers with a partner.

"Can Jennifer come out and work?"

1. Look at the cartoon. Do children normally dress like this?

2. When you were little, what did you want to be when you grew up?

3. Do you think it is important for children to think about their future careers? Why or why not?

B. Check (✔) whether you agree or disagree. Briefly discuss your answers with a partner.

Opinions about Children	Agree	Disagree
1. Children should spend their time playing.		
2. It is important for children to learn business writing skills.		
3. Children are too young to learn public speaking skills.		
4. Schools should teach children business skills.		
5. It is important for children to learn money management skills.		

2 | Active Previewing

A. Preview the newspaper article below by reading the first two paragraphs. Then answer these questions with a partner.

1. **Whom** (what group of people) is this article about?

2. **What** did they do?

3. **When** did they do it?

4. **Where** are they from?

B. Work as a class or in large groups. Try to say as many things as you can about the text.

C. Answer the questions with a partner.

1. What is the topic of this text?

2. What is the main idea of this text?

3 | Reading and Recalling

A. Read the text. Stop after each subtitled section and tell a partner two things you remember about it.

Young Dreams: Local Professionals Give Guidance to Adolescent Entrepreneurs

BY REBECCA MARKWAY

1 **Just Starting Out**
   A group of young entrepreneurs[1] in Baton Rouge recently had the opportunity to pitch their original business ideas to local professionals. They also had a chance to learn about developing business plans and how to market and advertise businesses.

2   As they waited to speak with the professionals, the entrepreneurs were understandably nervous, shuffling[2] uncomfortably and wiping their sweaty palms on their best clothes.

3   They were only 8 to 13 years old, after all.

4   The entrepreneurs and the professionals were brought together by Ann Broussard, founder and executive director of Young Entrepreneurs Succeeding (YES). The purpose of the YES program is to teach youths about business practices. The program had 50 applicants when it started in March 2000 and selected 15 students from four middle schools; it now has eleven participants. According to Broussard, it costs students $30 for three years and offers scholarships to low-income families. Participants must be good students, and their parents or guardians must sign a contract committing the students for three years.

5 **Sporting Goods, Snacks and Snowballs**
   The students in the YES program were a diverse lot, from aspiring[3] football and basketball players

continued

---

[1] **entrepreneur:** a person who starts a business, often by taking risks and chances

[2] **to shuffle:** to move one's feet without lifting them from the ground

[3] **aspiring:** having a strong desire or ambition

to pre-teen video game experts. Other participants included a cheerleader, a home-schooled student[4], and one very excited 8-year-old.

6   The business ideas were as diverse as the participants themselves were. Ricky Ray Jr., who plays many sports, came up with an interesting idea for a sporting goods store. Lee Slan, on the other hand, decided to pursue the food industry with LA's Snack Shop®. Jamb Mayberry, 13, presented her concept for a snowball and ice cream stand, Sunshine Snowballs.

7   For Mayberry, going into eighth grade at Glasgow Middle School, the snowball business is just the beginning of her professional career. She plans to attend Louisiana State University (high school first, of course) and possibly study fashion design or radiology.

8   **Looking Toward the Future**
Tommy Fronseca, vice president of Whitney Bank and chairman for the YES board of directors, said he sees the long-term value of early help for the budding entrepreneurs. In fact, Fronseca hopes the students will do business with Whitney Bank when they become successful adults with their own businesses.

9   Other YES board members who helped the students were Secretary Ruth Kohler of Custom Baskets-n-Gifts® and Public Awareness Committee Chair Virginia Pearson. And former Louisiana Governor Buddy Roemer, president and CEO of The Business Bank of Baton Rouge, acted as financial adviser. Roemer readily agreed to host the business briefing because he thought Broussard's idea was a "good fit" for his bank.

10 **Feedback from the Experts**
The panel of experts at the business briefing included LeAnne Weill, president of The Weill Agency, who enthusiastically counseled the students on advertising and marketing techniques along with helping them come up with their own unique brands and slogans.

11 "People will wear advertising," Weill told participant Kayla Williams while brainstorming for a brand name for Williams's custom slippers.

12 Participants received feedback on their business plans from Chris Russo-Love, publisher of *InRegister*. Russo-Love evaluated the writing style and format of the business plans and made sure each participant brought his or her main idea to the front of the plan.

13 Business etiquette and style were deemed important too. Dr. Shirley White of Success Images has been working with the participants on business behavior: greetings, handshakes, interpersonal non-verbal communication, eye contact, and dining etiquette. Kyle Hebert of McRae's Department Stores® gave the participants "dress for success" tips, and presented a mini fashion show highlighting what is appropriate to wear to an interview and how important personal image is in marketing a product.

14 The young participants soaked up[5] the tips and feedback. Many of them—even at such a young age—knew that this opportunity could benefit them for years to come.

15 And most of the participants already have big plans for their futures. Dean Loyd, father of 13-year-old Charlsey Loyd, remarked about his daughter, "She already has it in her head that she wants to be a millionaire by the time she's 30."

---

[4] **home-schooled student:** a student who is educated at home, often by a parent
[5] **to soak up:** to take in; to absorb quickly

B. Read the text again without pausing. Tell your partner two new things that you remember.

C. Work as a class or in large groups. Try to say as many things as you can about the text.

4 | Understanding the Text

A. Answer as many questions as you can without looking at the text. Discuss your answers with a partner.

1. What is the purpose of the Young Entrepreneurs Succeeding (YES) program?

   _____

   _____

2. How do young people qualify for participation in YES? _____

   _____

   _____

3. Who are the adults who participate in the YES program? _____

   _____

   _____

B. Complete the chart without looking at the text. Discuss your answers with a partner.

Skills or suggestions offered by the professionals to the students
1. *advertising and marketing techniques*
2.
3.

5 | Understanding the Topic and Main Idea

Text. Answer the questions and discuss your answers with a partner.

1. What is the topic of the text? _____

2. What is the main idea of the text? _____

   _____

   _____

3. Are your answers for the topic and the main idea here the same as the ones you determined after you previewed the text, or are your answers different? _____

6 | Understanding Pronouns and Possessive Adjectives

Answer the questions and discuss your answers with a partner.

1. In ¶1, what do these pronouns or possessive adjectives refer to?

   a. their (their original business ideas) _a group of young entrepreneurs_

   b. They (They also had a chance) _____

2. In ¶8, what do these pronouns or possessive adjectives refer to?

   a. he (he sees the long-term value) _____

   b. they (they become successful adults) _____

   c. their (their own businesses) _____

3. In ¶15, what do these pronouns or possessive adjectives refer to?

   a. their (for their futures) _____

   b. his (about his daughter) _____

   c. She (She already has) _____

REMEMBER

For more on *understanding possessive adjectives*, see page 72.

An **inference** is a logical conclusion that a reader makes based on the facts and/or opinions that he or she has read in a text. While facts and opinions are directly stated in an article, an inference is not.

Read the following sentence.

Ricky Ray Jr., who plays many sports, came up with an idea for a sporting goods store. (¶6)

This statement is in the text. In addition, the information can be proven, so it must be a fact. What inferences can we make from this statement? We know from the text that Ricky Ray Jr. plays sports and has an idea for a sporting goods store. We can therefore infer that Ricky Ray Jr. plays sports because he likes them, and that his liking for sports inspired his idea for a sporting goods store.

Distinguishing between fact, opinion, and inference

In order to decide if something is a **fact**, **opinion**, or **inference**, ask yourself:

1. Is it stated directly in the text?

   If it is, it is a fact or an opinion (go to number *2*). If not, it may be an inference.

2. If it is stated directly in the text, can it be tested or proven true or false?

   If it can, it is a fact. If it cannot, it is an opinion.

Ricky Ray Jr. plays many sports. (stated in ¶6, can be proven—it is a fact)

Ricky Ray Jr. had an interesting idea for a sporting goods store. (stated in ¶6, we cannot prove that the idea is interesting—it is an opinion)

Ricky Ray Jr. enjoys sports. (not stated in ¶6; it is an inference)

7 | Reading Critically—Facts, Opinions, and Inferences

A. **Making Inferences.** Answer the questions according to the text. Discuss your answers with a partner.

1. What inference can be made about ¶2?

   a. The entrepreneurs were nervous.

   b. The entrepreneurs were waiting to speak with the professionals.

   c. The entrepreneurs were nervous about speaking with the professionals.

2. What inference can be made about ¶7?

    a. Mayberry is going into eighth grade at Glasgow Middle School.

    b. Mayberry is interested in fashion.

    c. Mayberry plans to attend Louisiana State University.

3. What inference can be made about ¶10?

    a. LeAnne Weill enjoys working with the students.

    b. LeAnne Weill is the president of the Weill Agency.

    c. LeAnne Weill was on the panel of experts at the business briefing.

B. Distinguishing between Facts, Opinions, and Inferences. Write *F* for *Fact*, *O* for *Opinion*, or *I* for *Inference* according to the text. Discuss your answers with a partner.

_____I___ 1. Anne Broussard believes it is a good idea to teach young people about business.

_____ 2. The YES program had 50 applicants when it started in March 2000 and selected 15 students from four middle schools.

_____ 3. The students in the YES program were a diverse lot.

_____ 4. Ricky Ray Jr. is a good student.

_____ 5. Tommy Fronseca is chairman for the YES board of directors.

8 | Discussing the Issues

Answer the questions and discuss your answers with a partner.

1. What are some of the advantages of teaching young children business skills and strategies? Are there any disadvantages?

2. Do you think that—in addition to preparing the young participants for their future careers—the YES program might help them become better students? Why or why not?

3. What are three ways in which the local professionals could personally benefit from their participation in the YES program?

Text 2 | Are Businesses Out of Control?

1 | Getting Started

A. Answer the questions and briefly discuss your answers with a partner.

1. Do you think corporations and other large businesses are powerful?

2. Check (✔) the five qualities that you think are most important for a good corporation.

A good corporation...
☐ a. gives men and women equal opportunities.   ☐ f. is socially responsible.
☐ b. has a strong brand image/is well known.   ☐ g. is profitable.
☐ c. treats its employees well.   ☐ h. pays high salaries.
☐ d. has an interesting product or service.   ☐ i. provides job training to employees.
☐ e. is environmentally responsible.

3. Now rank the five qualities you checked from most important (1) to least important (5).

1. _____

2. _____

3. _____

4. _____

5. _____

B. Complete the chart with the qualities you checked in part *A*, indicating whether they show financial or social responsibility. Briefly discuss your answers with a partner.

Shows Financial Responsibility	Shows Social Responsibility

2 | Active Previewing

A. Preview the magazine article on the next page and tell a partner two things you remember about it.

B. Work as a class or in large groups. Try to say as many things as you can about the text.

C. Answer the questions with a partner.

1. What is the topic of this text?

2. What is the main idea of this text?

A. Read the text. Stop after each paragraph and tell a partner two things that you remember about it.

Is Corporate Social Responsibility an Oxymoron?

BY LOIS A. LEVIN AND ROBERT C. HINKLEY

1   The voices calling for corporate reform are getting louder. "Corporate social responsibility is an oxymoron[1]," according to a recent book and documentary film *The Corporation* by law professor Joel Bakan. He says corporations are like amoral[2] "psychopaths"—manipulative, incapable of being sensitive or remorseful, and, while causing tremendous damage to the environment and other elements of the public interest, they refuse to take responsibility for their behavior. Strong words, but they agree with those spoken by critics of corporate power throughout history.

2   Corporations are powerful institutions. They do not serve humanity well when their pursuit of profits leads to damaging strategies. They hurt the environment and violate human rights and the dignity[3] of employees. They endanger public health and safety and otherwise weaken the welfare of communities.

3   The people who run corporations are mostly decent human beings; many are responsible and active people in their communities. They care about the environment and other people, and they want to be recognized as good citizens.

Corporate abuse of the public interest is not due to flaws, or defects, in the characters of corporate personnel; it is due to a flaw in the rules under which the corporations themselves operate.

4   State laws that create corporations encourage behavior that managers and shareholders—people who own stock in a company—do not approve of in their personal lives. Those laws encourage managers to act as if shareholders are psychopaths—concerned only that their company makes more and more money without regard for the human or environmental costs. They allow managers to excuse themselves from the damage they do by claiming they are only doing what the law requires—promoting, or supporting, the interests of shareholders.

5   There are 80 million shareholders in the U.S. It is silly to presume that they have established a common goal to make money without regard for the public interest. Nonetheless, because of bad laws, good people in corporations (managers) make decisions on behalf of other good people (shareholders) that cause their institutions to engage in antisocial, or selfish, behavior.

6   Legislatures pass laws to control that behavior, but they are merely treating the symptoms of a problem while ignoring the underlying cause itself. A better solution, to prevent the problem from occurring in the first place, is to change the laws that create it.

7   People understand that doing well and doing good are not mutually exclusive. Shareholders are increasingly supporting decisions that address

continued

---

[1] **oxymoron:** a figure of speech that joins two terms that contradict each other, such as *bittersweet* and *larger half*

[2] **amoral:** not caring about what is right or wrong

[3] **dignity:** self-respect; self-esteem; pride

issues of corporate responsibility, even when those decisions support action that may not be in their short-term financial interest. For example, there is increasing evidence on a daily basis that the environment cannot protect itself. Many corporations are therefore taking steps to protect the environment and to adopt policies that enrich or improve the communities in which they operate. But these changes are slow and vulnerable to backsliding[4]. We cannot afford to wait decades to deal with climate change and other serious threats while corporations come around voluntarily.

8   Corporations have the potential to embrace human values if we, the citizens in whose name the corporate laws were enacted, demand it ourselves. To deal effectively with institutions that exhibit psychopathic behavior, it is essential to provide structure in the form of a code of conduct that clearly expresses expectations and standards, sets limits on such behavior, and provides appropriate punishments when the rules are broken—much as is done with psychopathic individuals.

9   We can begin by asking state legislators to enact the Model Code for Corporate Citizenship, which would add the following sentence to the corporate law: "The pursuit of profits must not come at the expense of the environment, human rights, public health and safety, the dignity of employees, or the welfare of communities."

10   Those 28 words will create new motivations and eliminate the excuse that corporate managers now use to justify antisocial corporate behavior—both to the world and to themselves. By making it clear to everyone in the corporation that protection of the public interest comes before making money, corporations will evolve and operate in more healthful and more holistic[5] ways that truly reflect the values of those who own them and those who work for them.

11   It is to be hoped that removing the excuse for behaving irresponsibly is all that will be needed for corporations to start taking responsibility for themselves. If not, the Code may be amended, or changed, to make its provisions legally enforceable. Either way, the Code will have a beneficial effect on corporate decision-making. The sooner we make this change, the better.

> Corporations have the potential to embrace human values if we, the citizens in whose name the corporate laws were enacted, demand it ourselves.

---

[4] **to backslide:** to return to wrongdoing; to drop to a lower level
[5] **holistic:** describes something in which the whole is more important than the parts

B. Read the text again without pausing. Tell your partner two new things that you remember.

C. Work as a class or in large groups. Try to say as many things as you can about the text.

4 | Understanding the Text

A. Answer as many questions as you can without looking at the text. Discuss your answers with a partner.

1. According to Joel Bakan, what are corporations like? _____

_____

_____

2. What are the people like who run the corporations? _____

_____

_____

3. What solution is proposed for correcting corporations' behavior? _____

_____

_____

B. Check (✔) all of the phrases that apply to a socially responsible company, according to the text.

☐ 1. cares about the environment

☐ 2. cares about public health and safety

☐ 3. engages in antisocial behavior

☐ 4. enriches the community in which it operates

☐ 5. is concerned about making money

☐ 6. is manipulative

☐ 7. protects human rights

☐ 8. refuses to take responsibility

☐ 9. violates the dignity of employees

5 | Understanding the Topic, Main Idea, and Supporting Details

A. Text. Answer the questions and discuss your answers with a partner.

1. What is the topic of the text? _____

2. What is the main idea of the text? _____

_____

_____

3. Are your answers for the topic and the main idea here the same as the ones you determined after you previewed the text, or are your answers different? _____

B. Paragraphs. Answer the questions and write *MI* for *Main Idea*. Discuss your answers with a partner.

1. What is the topic of ¶2? _____

2. What is the main idea of ¶2?

    a. _____ Corporations are powerful.

    b. _____ Corporations do not serve humanity when their pursuit of profit leads to damaging strategies.

    c. _____ Corporations are guilty of violating human rights.

3. What are the supporting details for ¶2? _____

_____

4. What is the topic of ¶3? _____

5. What is the main idea of ¶3?

    a. _____ The people who run corporations are mostly decent and responsible.

    b. _____ Many people who run corporations care about the environment and other people.

    c. _____ The rules under which corporations operate are flawed.

6. What are the supporting details for ¶3? _____

_____

7. What is the topic of ¶4? _____

8. What is the main idea of ¶4? _____

_____

9. What are the supporting details for ¶4? _____

_____

VOCABULARY STRATEGY Understanding Reflexive Pronouns

Reflexive pronouns are used when the noun or pronoun is doing something to or for itself. They are also sometimes used when the writer wants to emphasize that someone or something did an action himself or itself. A reflexive pronoun is formed by a personal pronoun +**self** or **selves: myself, yourself, herself, himself, itself, ourselves, yourselves,** and **themselves.**

Read the sentences.

1. It is due to a flaw in the rules under which the corporation *themselves* operate. (¶3)

   Who or what does *themselves* refer to? *Themselves* refers to *corporations*. The writer is emphasizing that the corporations operate under their own rules.

2. They allow managers to excuse *themselves* from the damage they do... (¶4)

   Who or what does *themselves* refer to? *Themselves* refers to *managers*. The writer is emphasizing that the people who excuse managers from the damage they do are the managers.

6 | Understanding Reflexive Pronouns

Answer the questions and discuss your answers with a partner.

1. In ¶6, what does *itself* (the underlying cause itself) refer to? _____

   _____

2. In ¶7, what does *itself* (cannot protect itself) refer to? _____

   _____

3. In ¶8, what does *ourselves* (demand it ourselves) refer to? _____

   _____

4. In ¶10, what does *themselves* (and to themselves) refer to? _____

   _____

5. In ¶11, what does *themselves* (taking responsibility for themselves) refer to? _____

   _____

7 | Understanding Vocabulary in Context—Synonyms

Write the synonym for each word or phrase according to the text.

1. flaws (¶3) _____

2. shareholders (¶4) _____

3. to promote (¶4) _____

4. antisocial (¶5) _____

5. to amend (¶11) _____

8 | Reading Critically—Facts, Opinions, and Inferences

Write *F* for *Fact*, *O* for *Opinion*, or *I* for *Inference* according to the text. Discuss your answers with a partner.

   _F_   1. Joel Bakan believes in corporate reform.

   _____   2. The people who run corporations are mostly decent human beings.

   _____   3. There are 80 million shareholders in the U.S.

   _____   4. Shareholders sometimes find corporate responsibility more important than financial interest.

   _____   5. Corporations have the potential to embrace human values if we the citizens demand it ourselves.

9 | Discussing the Issues

Answer the questions and discuss your answers with a partner.

1. How might a corporation justify emptying poisonous chemicals into the air?

2. How would you react if you discovered that the pollution from a nearby factory represented a serious danger to you and your family?

3. Do you agree with the opinions expressed in the text, or do you feel that corporations should be allowed to choose freely how they address issues of corporate social responsibility? Why?

Text 3 | The Cycle of Motivation

1 | Getting Started

Complete the chart based on how you feel when you receive positive or negative feedback from a teacher or boss. Use the words in the box.

| angry | disinterested in work | nervous and hesitant |
| confident | happy | embarrased | motivated to work harder |

Positive feedback	Negative feedback

GRAPHICS Previewing Diagrams

Diagrams give a visual idea of information. **Preview** diagrams by reading the title and any subtitles, and then looking at the diagram as a whole. If there are few words, read everything and focus on the content.

2 | Active Previewing

Preview the diagrams on the next page and then answer the questions. Discuss your answers with a partner.

1. What are the titles of these two diagrams?

2. What is the topic of these diagrams?

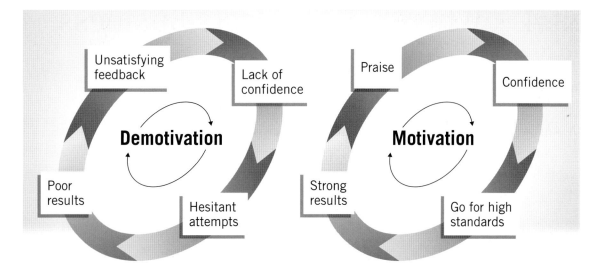

3 | Understanding the Graphics

Answer the questions according to the graphics. Discuss your answers with a partner.

1. What leads to unsatisfying feedback? _poor results_

2. What does lack of confidence lead to? _____

3. What leads to poor results? _____

4. What leads to praise? _____

5. What does praise lead to? _____

4 | Reading Critically—Facts, Opinions, and Inferences

Write *F* for *Fact*, *O* for *Opinion*, or *I* for *Inference* according to the graphics. Discuss your answers with a partner.

___F___ **1.** Poor results are part of the Demotivation diagram.

_____ **2.** Motivated people have greater success at school or work.

_____ **3.** Praise is part of the Motivation diagram.

_____ **4.** Demotivated people usually have poor results.

_____ **5.** Praise leads to confidence.

5 | Discussing the Issues

Answer the questions and discuss your answers with a partner.

1. Think of a time when you received praise for your work in school or at your job. How did it make you feel?

2. Think of a time when you received criticism or abuse for your work in school or at your job. How did it make you feel?

3. How might the information in the diagrams affect the way you give feedback to others?

Text 4 | When Beauty Meets Business

1 | Getting Started

A. Answer the questions and briefly discuss your answers with a partner.

a b c d

e f g h

1. Do you use cosmetics?

2. Look at the photos. Circle all of the items that are sold at cosmetics stores.

3. What other items are sold at cosmetics stores?

B. Complete the chart and briefly discuss your answers with a partner.

An entrepreneur needs these qualities in order to be successful
1.
2.
3.
An entrepreneur should do these things in order to be successful
1.
2.
3.

2 | Active Previewing

A. Preview the academic text below and tell a partner two things you remember about it.

B. Work as a class or in large groups. Try to say as many things as you can about the text.

C. Answer the questions with a partner.

1. What is the topic of this text?

2. What is the main idea of this text?

REMEMBER

Preview academic texts by reading the title, the subtitles, the first sentence of each paragraph, and the final sentence of the text. Preview longer academic texts a second time.

For more about *previewing academic texts*, see page 3.

3 | Reading and Recalling

A. Read the text. Stop after each paragraph and tell a partner two things that you remember about it.

Putting on a New Face

The Creation of a Caring Corporation

by Cynthia Kersey

1   No one who has ever followed a dream has taken a direct path and arrived at his or her destination effortlessly and on time. Following a dream can be a bumpy road full of twists and turns and occasional roadblocks. The journey requires changes and adjustments in both thought and action, not just once, but over and over. Anita Roddick, the founder of The Body Shop®, used creativity to overcome challenges that would have stopped the vast majority of new business owners. She broke just about every rule of business when she started The Body Shop®, and she continued to break the rules until she recently retired.

2   Of course, such irreverence[1] has its consequences. In Anita's case, the consequences read like this: The Body Shop® now has more than 1,500 stores around the world, is worth over $500 million, and has influenced the products and marketing of all its major competitors. And those are just the consequences in the business arena. The Body Shop® is also a powerfully effective vehicle for social and environmental awareness and change; as far as Anita is concerned, that is the most important consequence of all.

3   From the moment in 1976 when Anita first conceived the idea of opening a shop to sell naturally based cosmetics, she was thinking in a most unbusinesslike manner. Most entrepreneurs set out to create a company with growth potential that will make them wealthy someday. Anita was just looking for a way to feed herself and her two children, while her husband, also a maverick[2], was away on a two-year adventure, riding a horse from Argentina to New York.

4   Anita's first challenge was to find a cosmetics manufacturer to produce her products. No one she approached had ever heard of jojoba oil or aloe vera gel, and they all thought that cocoa butter had something to do with chocolate. Although she didn't realize it at the time, Anita had discovered a market that was just about to explode: young female consumers who would prefer their cosmetics to be produced in a

continued

---

[1] **irreverence:** disrespect
[2] **maverick:** a person who resists the regular rules of society

cruelty-free and environmentally responsible manner. When manufacturers failed to have the same vision as she did, Anita found a small herbalist who could do the work she required.

5 Since Anita was not the typical entrepreneur, she saw no disadvantages to starting her company with almost no finances. To save money, she bottled her cosmetics in the same inexpensive plastic containers hospitals use for urine samples, encouraging her customers to bring the containers back for refills. Because Anita couldn't afford to have labels printed, she hand printed them herself with the help of some friends. Her packaging couldn't have turned out better if she'd planned it that way. With the improvised packaging, her product now had the same natural, earthy image as the cosmetics themselves.

6 Anita opened the first branch of The Body Shop® in her hometown of Brighton, England. When she first opened, neighboring business owners and shop owners made bets among themselves on how long the store would last. Less amused were the owners of local funeral parlors[3] who insisted she change the shop's name. No one, they complained, would hire a funeral director located near a place called "The Body Shop®." She stuck to her guns and the name stayed.

7 The first store was only minimally successful. Nevertheless, Anita decided to move ahead with a second one. The bank questioned the wisdom of her plan and refused a loan. So she found a friend of a friend who was willing to lend her the equivalent of $6,400 in exchange for 50 percent ownership of The Body Shop®. Today that person is worth $140 million. Signing over half of her business was the only real mistake Anita ever made.

8 However, this decision wasn't the only one that looked like a mistake. Here are three more: Anita has never advertised even when she opened shops in the United States. People told her it was suicide to enter a new market without massive advertising support. In addition, she doesn't sell in any outlet other than The Body Shop® stores—the exception being that some of her Asian stores are located within department stores. Finally, she decided early on that her shops would be a spark for change, not just in the business world, but in the world at large.

9 These decisions turned out to be some of the most inspired "mistakes" in the history of retailing. Even though Anita has never paid for advertising, her unconventional ideas have inspired hundreds of articles and interviews, which have generated tremendous publicity. Her first shop in New York was packed with customers from the day it opened. At one point, a thirty-five-year-old woman on roller skates threw up her arms and shouted, "Hallelujah! You're here at last." So much for advertising. Nowadays, a new branch of The Body Shop® opens somewhere in the world every two and a half days.

10 Occasionally, Anita has had trouble opening stores in shopping malls. But having a past that was filled with challenges, Anita is accustomed to coming up with creative solutions. For instance, when one mall refused to lease her space, she organized every mail-order customer within a 110-mile radius to write letters to the management of that mall. Within a few months, a branch of The Body Shop® was open.

11 Anita also had this nonconformist idea of putting ideals ahead of profit. From the start, Anita wanted not just to change the faces of her customers but to change the entire face of business. She envisioned a company that was socially responsible and compassionate. "I see the human spirit playing a big role in business…the sole focus does not have to be on making money. It can be a human enterprise that people feel genuinely good about."

12 Some of the raw materials for Anita's beauty products are collected by groups of people in underdeveloped regions, thus creating an income for them. The Body Shop® has started campaigns to save the whales, ban animal testing in the cosmetics industry, help the homeless, and protect the rain forests. Loyal customers have eagerly supported all of these campaigns.

13 Employees of The Body Shop® are actively involved in these efforts. Some employees,

continued

---

[3] **funeral parlor:** a place where dead people are prepared for burial or cremation

continued

for example, went to Romania to help rebuild orphanages[4]. Furthermore, each month, employees receive a half day off with pay to volunteer in the community. In the stores, customers are encouraged to register to vote, recycle their plastic cosmetics containers, and bring their own shopping bags to save paper and plastic. Because of all these activities, people have suggested Anita's company should really be called "The Body and Soul Shop." Customers come out not only looking good but also feeling good.

14   "Business as usual" isn't part of Anita Roddick's make up. But as far as she's concerned, doing what is not usual has made all the difference.

15   When The Body Shop® has been in trouble, Anita said that what saved them over and over was their willingness to recognize what wasn't working and quickly identify a new way to approach a problem. This is a crucial strategy because everyone who starts a business is going to face challenges[5]. Things never work out exactly as intended, and creativity will play a key role in enabling a new business owner to conquer daily battles.

---

[4] **orphanage:** an institution that takes care of children who have no parents
[5] **to face a challenge:** to be confronted with a difficult situation or problem

B. Read the text again without pausing. Tell your partner two new things that you remember.

C. Work as a class or in large groups. Try to say as many things as you can about the text.

4 | Understanding the Text

A. Answer as many questions as you can without looking at the text. Discuss your answers with a partner.

1. Who is Anita Roddick? _____

2. What does Roddick consider to be the most important consequence of The Body Shop®?

   _____

   _____

3. What kinds of products does The Body Shop® sell? _____

   _____

4. Why did Roddick open The Body Shop®? _____

   _____

5. What does Roddick say has saved The Body Shop® from various troubles over time?

   _____

   _____

B. Complete the chart without looking at the text. Discuss your answers with a partner.

Anita Roddick's business is different because...
1.
2.
3.

5 | Understanding the Topic, Main Idea, and Supporting Details

A. Text. Answer the questions and discuss your answers with a partner.

1. What is the topic of the text? _____

2. What is the main idea of the text? _____

_____

_____

3. Are your answers for the topic and the main idea here the same as the ones you determined after you previewed the text, or are your answers different? _____

B. Paragraphs. Answer the questions and write *MI* for *Main Idea*. Discuss your answers with a partner.

1. What is the topic of ¶2? _____

2. What is the main idea of ¶2?

   a. _____ The Body Shop® now has more than 1,500 stores around the world.

   b. _____ Roddick's irreverence has had consequences.

   c. _____ Roddick's irreverence has made The Body Shop® a successful and responsible business.

3. What are the supporting details for ¶2? _____

_____

_____

_____

4. What is the topic of ¶5? _____

5. What is the main idea of ¶5? _____

_____

6. What are the supporting details for ¶5? _____

_____

_____

7. What is the topic of ¶11? _____

8. What is the main idea of ¶11? _____

_____

9. What are the supporting details for ¶11? _____

_____

_____

6 | Understanding Pronouns and Possessive Adjectives

Answer the questions and discuss your answers with a partner.

1. In ¶3, what do these pronouns or possessive adjectives refer to?

a. she (she was thinking) _Anita_____

b. them (make them wealthy) _____

c. herself (to feed herself) _____

d. her (her two small children) _____

2. In ¶4, what do these pronouns or possessive adjectives refer to?

a. she (she approached) _____

b. she (she didn't realize it) _____

c. their (their cosmetics) _____

3. In ¶5, what do these pronouns or possessive adjectives refer to?

a. her (her company) _____

b. them (hand printed them) _____

c. themselves (the cosmetics themselves) _____

7 | Understanding Vocabulary in Context—Collocations

Select the best meaning for each collocation according to the text.

_____ **1.** to set out to (do something) (¶3)

_____ **2.** to stick to one's guns (¶6)

_____ **3.** to sign over (¶7)

_____ **4.** to be packed with (something) (¶9)

_____ **5.** to come up with (something) (¶10)

a. to be full of people or things

b. to refuse to change one's mind

c. to give ownership, or partial ownership, to someone legally

d. to create

e. to go forward with a plan, usually for the first time

8 | Reading Critically—Making Inferences

Complete the chart according to the text. Discuss your answers with a partner.

Roddick's Qualities	Example from the text
1. daring	Roddick decided to go into business on her own in order to feed herself and her two children.
2. imaginative	
3. strong-willed	
4. caring	
5. flexible	

9 | Discussing the Issues

Answer the questions and discuss your answers with a partner.

1. What do you think of Anita Roddick's approach to her business?

2. If you were going to start a business, how would your approach be similar to or different from Roddick's?

3. Roddick claims that when The Body Shop® has been in trouble, what has saved them is their ability to recognize what wasn't working and quickly identify a new way to approach the problem. Do you feel this approach might be valuable outside business? Why or why not?

Putting It On Paper

A. Write a five-paragraph essay on one of these topics.

1. Describe three advantages or disadvantages of being a socially responsible company.

2. Describe three advantages or disadvantages of teaching children the basics of business.

Steps for your essay

a. In your first paragraph, clearly state your opinion about your topic and your general reason or reasons why.

b. Your second, third, and fourth paragraphs should each contain an advantage or disadvantage that relates to your topic.

c. In your final paragraph, summarize the ideas you state in your essay.

B. Exchange essays with a partner. First, read your partner's essay and answer the questions on the checklist. Then give feedback to your partner.

> **NOTE**
>
> Each of your paragraphs should contain a main idea that is supported by details—facts, data, examples—that prove or illustrate your main idea. For more on *supporting details*, see page 77.

✔ CHECKLIST

1. Does ¶1 show your partner's opinion about the topic?
2. Do the three body paragraphs support the topic?
3. Does the final paragraph summarize the ideas contained in the essay?
4. Does each paragraph contain a main idea?
5. Do the details of each paragraph support the main idea?
6. Do your partner's advantages or disadvantages persuade you?
7. Is there any information in the essay that is not related to your partner's thesis? If yes, please underline it on your partner's essay, and write it below:

_____

_____

_____

_____

_____

C. Revise your essay based on your partner's feedback.

Taking It Online | Social Responsibility

A. With a partner, use the Internet to research socially responsible and socially irresponsible companies.

1. Discuss with your partner the qualities you think make a company socially responsible.

2. Use Google (www.google.com) or another major search engine to begin your online search.

3. Search for websites with information about two companies that meet your criteria for a socially responsible company and two companies that do not. You may find some of these terms useful:

company	waste/wasteful
corporation	environmental/-ly
ethical/unethical	responsible/irresponsible
honest/dishonest	labor practice
pollutant	

> **ONLINE TIP**
>
> Search with a simple form or word part for more inclusive results: "corporation" (not "corporations").

4. Preview the websites.

B. Complete the table with the information you find.

Socially Responsible Companies	
Name:	Name:
Website:	Website:
Type of business:	Type of business:
Reason:	Reason:
Socially Irresponsible Companies	
Name:	Name:
Website:	Website:
Type of business:	Type of business:
Reason:	Reason:

C. Following up. Discuss your research with the class or in small groups. Think of three actions you could take to support the socially responsible companies or challenge the socially irresponsible companies.

Chapter 7

The Global Diet

Answer the questions and briefly discuss your answers with a partner.

1. Do you think you have a healthful diet?

2. What is considered a healthful diet in your family?

3. Look at the photos. What health risks or benefits, if any, do you think may be associated with eating any of these foods or food products?

Text 1 | The Mediterranean Diet

1 | Getting Started

A. Answer the questions and briefly discuss your answers with a partner.

pasta

cous-cous

hamburger and fries

sushi

salad

grilled fish, rice, and veggies

1. Look at the photos. Have you eaten any of these dishes?

2. Are any of these dishes from a particular country or region?

3. Which of these dishes are healthful, and which are not healthful? Why?

4. Which regions of the world have the most healthful diets?

B. Complete the chart and briefly discuss your answers with a partner.

Healthful food	This food is healthful because . . .
1.	
2.	
3.	

2 | Active Previewing

A. Preview the newspaper article below by reading the first two paragraphs. Then with a partner, answer as much as you can without looking at the text.

1. Whom (what group of people) is this article about?

2. What are they doing?

3. Where are they from?

B. Work as a class or in large groups. Try to name as many things as you can about the text.

C. Answer the questions with a partner.

1. What is the topic of this text?

2. What is the main idea of this text?

3 | Reading and Recalling

A. Read the text. Stop after each subtitled section and tell a partner two things that you remember about it.

Mediterranean Diet Linked to Longer Life

BY SALYNN BOYLES
Reviewed by Michael Smith, MD

1   There is more evidence that eating like a villager on the Isle of Crete can help you live longer. A study examining eating patterns in nine European countries found that people who ate a traditional Mediterranean diet lived longer than those who didn't.

2   Researchers say a healthy man of 60 who follows the diet, which is rich in fruits and vegetables and low in meat and dairy, can expect to live a year longer than a man the same age who doesn't follow the diet. "A year may not sound like much to some people," study researcher Dimitrios Trichopoulos, MD, PhD tells *WebMD*. "But I'm in my mid 60s, and it sounds pretty good to me."

3   **Living to 100**
    Physiologist Ancel Keys was both the world's best known champion of the Mediterranean diet and its best advertisement. Keys was the first to notice, more than half a century ago, that heart disease was rare in Mediterranean areas like Greece and southern Italy, where olive oil and red wine were dietary staples[1] and people ate plenty of fruits and vegetables.

4   Keys died late last year at the age of 100, still active and doing nutrition research until the last few years of his life. In an interview with *WebMD* in 2000, he lamented[2] the fact that the typical meat, cheese, and pasta-heavy dishes Americans

continued

---

[1] **dietary staple:** a basic part of a culture's diet, such as rice or bread

[2] **to lament:** to express grief or sadness about something

encounter in Italian restaurants have little in common with traditional Mediterranean fare[3]. "The Mediterranean diet was nearly vegetarian, with fish and very little meat, and was rich in green vegetables," he said adding that something got lost in the translation from Italy to the U.S. "They may call it Italian, but it's very different from the food we studied."

5 **Eating Mediterranean**

The newly published study involved more than 74,000 healthy men and women aged 60 and older living in Denmark, France, Germany, Greece, Italy, the Netherlands, Spain, Sweden, and the United Kingdom. Study participants were asked about their diets, medical and smoking histories, exercise patterns, and other relevant health information. Researchers measured how closely they stuck to a Mediterranean-style diet using a special scale developed by the researchers. The findings are reported in the April 8 issue of the *British Medical Journal*.

6 Eating a Mediterranean-style diet was linked to a longer life. The largest association was seen in Greece and southern Italy, where people stuck more closely to the diet.

7 **Mediterranean Diet: More Than Olive Oil**

Trichopoulos says there is no single component of the Mediterranean diet that holds the key to longer life. Though the mantra[4] of Mediterranean eating could be "olive oil good, saturated fats bad," there is more to it than that. "In this case, the total is better than the sum of the parts," he says. "You can't point to one thing and say that is what does it."

People who follow traditional Mediterranean diets:

• Eat mostly plant foods, including fruits, vegetables, beans, whole grains, and nuts.

• Eat fish often, but eat other animal-based foods such as red meat, poultry, and dairy sparingly.

• Drink alcohol in moderation—no more than one drink a day for women and no more than two drinks a day for men. While many believe that red wine offers health advantages over other forms of alcohol, Trichopoulos says that is still not clear. One drink equals 1.5 ounces of liquor (whiskey, gin, vodka, etc.), 5 ounces of wine, or 12 ounces of beer.

• Don't limit fat consumption, as long as fats are derived[5] from plants, not animals, and are not overly refined. Trichopoulos says olive oil is the best fat, but canola and soybean oils are also good.

8 **Going to Extremes**

Trichopoulos says the current mania for low-carbohydrate eating in the U.S. incorporates some elements of Mediterranean eating but not others. "Americans tend to go to extremes when it comes to eating, and right now they hate carbohydrates and love protein," he says. "Lowering carbohydrates is probably a good thing, but too much meat-based protein is not."

9 Nutrition researcher Alice Lichtenstein, DSc, is a strong proponent of Mediterranean eating. But she worries that people will lose sight of the fact that there is more to good health than what you eat.

"Two-thirds of Americans are overweight or obese," she says. "If everyone adopted this diet but did not change anything else, it is unlikely that they would reap the benefits." In other words, getting regular exercise and limiting calories, no matter what form they come in, is just as important as following a particular diet.

10 "There is no simple fix," she says. "You really have to think about the whole package. Not just what you are eating, but how much you are eating and whether you are moving. There are no shortcuts to good health."

---

[3] **fare:** food and drink that are regularly consumed

[4] **mantra:** an important word or phrase that is said or sung repeatedly

[5] **to derive:** to obtain from a specific source

B. Read the text again without pausing. Tell your partner two new things that you remember.

C. Work as a class or in large groups. Try to name as many things as you can about the text.

4 | Understanding the Text

A. Answer as many questions as you can without looking at the text. Discuss your answers with a partner.

1. What did Ancel Keyes think about the Mediterranean diet? _____

   _____

2. What is a "Mediterranean diet"? _____

   _____

3. What did the results of the study in Europe show? _____

   _____

B. Complete the chart according to the text. Discuss your answers with a partner.

People who follow a traditional Mediterranean diet...
1. eat mostly plant foods (fruits, vegetables, beans, whole grains, nuts, etc.).
2.
3.
4.

5 | Understanding the Topic and Main Idea

Text. Answer the questions and discuss your answers with a partner.

1. What is the topic of the text? _____

   _____

2. What is the main idea of the text? _____

   _____

   _____

3. Are your answers for the topic and the main idea here the same as the ones you determined after you previewed the text, or are your answers different? _____

Demonstrative pronouns point to and identify nouns or pronouns. They can function as subjects, objects, or objects of a preposition. The singular demonstrative pronouns are **this** and **that**, and the plural demonstrative pronouns are **these** and **those**.

Read the following sentences.

1. You can't point to one thing and say *that* is what does it. (¶7)

   The demonstrative pronoun *that* refers to the noun phrase *one thing*. In other words, the first sentence could read: "You can't point to one thing and say the one thing is what does it."

   Note: Do not confuse demonstrative pronouns with adjectives. Adjectives modify nouns, whereas demonstrative pronouns *represent* or *replace* the nouns. Read the sentence.

2. In *this* case, the total is better than the sum of the parts..." (¶7)

   This is an adjective that modifies the noun *case*.

6 | Understanding Demonstrative Pronouns

Write what each demonstrative pronoun refers to according to the text.

1. those (those who didn't) (¶1) _____

2. that (there is more to it than that) (¶7) _____

3. that (that is still not clear) (¶7) _____

7 | Understanding Vocabulary in Context—Context Clues

Select the best meaning for each word or phrase according to the text.

1. sparingly (¶7)

   a. in equal amounts   b. in large amounts   c. in small amounts

2. in moderation (¶7)

   a. in limited amounts   b. a lot   c. never

3. refined (¶7)

   a. derived from plants   b. artificially purified   c. natural

8 | Reading Critically—Facts, Opinions, and Inferences

Write F for *Fact*, O for *Opinion*, or I for *Inference* according to the text. Discuss your answers with a partner.

___F___ 1. A study found that people who ate a traditional Mediterranean diet lived longer than those who didn't.

_____ 2. Ancel Keys was the world's best known champion of the Mediterranean diet.

_____ 3. Keys wished the food served in American-Italian restaurants were more like traditional Mediterranean fare.

_____ 4. Low-carbohydrate diets are not the most healthful diets.

_____ 5. Two-thirds of Americans are overweight or obese.

9 | Discussing the Issues

Answer the questions and discuss your answers with a partner.

1. Would you change the way you eat in order to have better health? Why or why not?

2. How do you think this text might persuade someone to make any changes in his or her diet?

3. In your opinion, what is the best way to stay healthy?

Text 2 | The Joy of Soy

1 | Getting Started

A. Answer the questions and briefly discuss your answers with a partner.

1. Check (✔) the foods that will help to build strong muscles and give the body long, sustained energy (protein-rich foods).

☐ a. fish and shellfish

☐ b. beans

☐ c. fruits

☐ d. tofu and soy-based foods

☐ e. butter and oil

☐ f. cheese, yogurt, and other dairy products

☐ g. vegetables

☐ h. eggs

☐ i. bread, rice, and noodles

☐ j. lamb, beef, and pork

2. Do you eat a lot of protein-rich foods?

3. What do you think can happen if a person doesn't have enough proteins in his diet?

B. Complete the chart and then briefly discuss your answers with a partner.

Diseases common to older people
1.
2.
3.
Recommendations for avoiding these diseases
1.
2.
3.

Skimming is letting your eyes glide through a text as you read quickly. A reader **skims** a text when he or she wants to get a general idea about the information contained in the text but does not need to know full details.

For example, skimming is useful when a reader:

    a. wants to see if the full text is worth reading.

    b. wants to find key facts about a subject.

    c. wants to know the outcome or status of a current event.

    d. is writing a term paper and has to look through dozens of sources for useful information.

    e. wants to know which movies or restaurants the local newspaper recommends and why.

    f. has only a few minutes to review a business report before a meeting.

    g. is reading a story and cannot wait to find out what happens in the end.

To skim:

1. Read the title and any subtitles.

2. Read the first one or two paragraphs.

3. Read the first and/or last sentence of the other paragraphs.

4. Look quickly over the body of the other paragraphs, reading only a few words here and there. You may note names, places, dates and numbers, and words in bold or italic print.

5. Read the last paragraph.

2 | Skimming

A. Skim the magazine article on the next page in three minutes or less. Then answer the questions with a partner.

1. According to the text, what is an easy thing to do in order to improve one's health?

2. What are two of the products shown in the photograph?

3. What are two diseases soy may have a positive effect on?

4. How many grams of soy should one try to incorporate into one's diet?

5. In what two countries is soy consumption high?

> **NOTE**
> Skimming a text will help you identify the topic and main idea of a text. There is no need for a separate preview.

B. Work as a class or in large groups. Try to name as many things as you can about the text.

C. Answer the questions with a partner.

1. What is the topic of this text?

2. What is the main idea of this text?

3 | Reading and Recalling

A. Read the text. Stop after each paragraph and tell a partner two things that you remember about it.

Soy: It Does a Body Good

BY PSYCHOLOGY TODAY STAFF

1   Eating soy, it now appears, is one of the simplest things we can do to boost[1] our health. Once revered as a sacred crop in China, soybeans are one of the richest plant sources of protein. In fact, the World Health Organization considers it on a par with meat and dairy proteins. And not only is this low-fat dietary protein great news for vegetarians or dieters, but a growing body of research also indicates that soy may help prevent many chronic diseases.

2   Many of soy's therapeutic benefits are believed to come from its vast stores[2] of bioactive plant chemicals called isoflavones. These are able to stabilize estrogen, a female hormone necessary for normal growth and development. They adjust the hormone's effects when levels are too high or low.

3   To get the most out of soy, health experts suggest eating whole foods like tofu, soymilk, and tempeh because they contain higher levels of isoflavones than supplements[3] do. Fortunately, there are now a variety of soy and tofu products that are both convenient and tasty. Both fresh and long-conservation soymilk are easy to find in many supermarkets, and soymilk can be used in place of cow's milk for both drinking and cooking.

4   The biggest news is that soy reduces cholesterol and protects against heart disease. This was demonstrated in an analysis of 38 studies published in the prestigious *New England Journal of Medicine*. The analysis showed that eating soy lowers total levels of cholesterol by 10% and LDL or "bad" cholesterol by 13%. In 1999, the Food

Tofu, soy sauce, and soy milk are just some of the products made with soy.

and Drug Administration gave soy the green light, stating definitively that eating 25 grams of soy protein each day as part of a low-fat, low-cholesterol diet reduces the risk of heart disease. Recently, the American Heart Association revised its dietary guidelines to recommend soy as part of a heart-healthy diet.

5   While research on other diseases isn't yet conclusive, scientists believe that soy may also help protect against osteoporosis, a disease that pro-

---

[1] **to boost:** to increase; to assist in the progress of; to better

[2] **store:** great number or quantity; supply

[3] **supplement:** something that is added to complete something else that has a lack; here: vitamin, mineral, enzyme, etc. that would be taken to fulfill a nutritional lack

continued

gressively decreases bone density. Although both men and women are susceptible, women are especially at risk. They are four times more likely to be affected. A 1998 study published in the American Journal of Clinical Nutrition found that postmenopausal women who ate 40 grams of soy protein a day significantly increased the bone density in their spines. And a University of Iowa study found that women who consumed soy maintained bone density, while those whose diet didn't include isoflavones actually lost bone density. "The isoflavones in soy are identical to a drug called Ipriflavone, a synthetic isoflavone used for bone loss, so there's reason to think that isoflavones will do something for bone health," says Mark Messina, Ph.D., an adjunct associate professor of nutrition at Loma Linda University in California and former program director for the National Cancer Institute (NCI). "In general, if you substitute soy for animal protein, you'll lose less calcium from your bones because animal protein causes calcium loss."

> "I suspect that when the ongoing trials are completed, we'll see that soy may protect against cancer."

6   According to the NCI, soy is believed to coax[4] cancerous cells to revert to normal. It may also prevent tumors from obtaining nutrients and block free radicals. These are compounds that normally attack bacteria and viruses, and they can damage healthy cells. "There are several potent anti-cancer compounds in soy," says Clare Hasler, Ph.D., executive director of the Functional Foods for Health program at the University of Illinois. "I suspect that when the ongoing trials are completed, we'll see that soy may protect against cancer." Because of its estrogenic properties, soy appears most effective against hormone-related cancers like prostate and colon cancers. Another study presented at the same symposium on soy found that soy reduced tumors by 40% to 60% in mice with prostate or bladder cancer.

7   Epidemiological[5] studies suggest that soy also protects against breast cancer, and researchers often point to Japan and China where soy consumption is high and breast cancer rates are low. Even so, scientists recently discovered that, because consuming soy promotes breast cell growth, doing so later in life may actually raise the risk of breast cancer for postmenopausal women with a personal or family history of the disease.

8   Most supermarkets typically carry a wide variety of soy foods like soy nuts, snack bars, and instant shakes. These are all ready to grab for people on the go. One easy and satisfying way to include 25 grams of soy protein in one's daily diet is to down a shake made with instant soy protein powder. Other convenience foods like soy-based burgers, hot dogs, deli meats, and bacon have a taste and texture that is very similar to real meats. For a better diet, think health and think soy!

---

[4] **to coax:** to change or adjust something toward a specific goal
[5] **epidemiology:** a branch of medicine that studies disease in specific populations

B. Read the text again without pausing. Tell your partner two new things that you remember.

C. Work as a class or in large groups. Try to name as many things as you can about the text.

4 | Understanding the Text

A. Answer as many questions as you can without looking at the text. Discuss your answers with a partner.

1. What is soy? _____

2. Are isoflavones good or bad? _____

3. Where can one buy soy products? _____

B. Complete the chart according to the text. Discuss your answers with a partner.

Benefits of consuming soy
1. *Soy is a good source of protein.*
2.
3.
4.
5.

5 | Understanding the Topic, Main Idea, and Supporting Details

A. Text. Answer the questions and discuss your answers with a partner.

1. What is the topic of the text? _____

   _____

2. What is the main idea of the text? _____

   _____

   _____

3. Are your answers for topic and main idea here the same as those you determined after you skimmed the text, or are your answers different? _____

B. Paragraphs. Answer the questions and discuss your answers with a partner.

1. What is the topic of ¶2? _____

2. What is the main idea of ¶2? _____

   _____

3. What are the supporting details for ¶2? _____

   _____

4. What is the topic of ¶4? _____

5. What is the main idea of ¶4? _____

   _____

6. What are the supporting details for ¶4? _____

_____

_____

7. What is the topic of ¶5? _____

8. What is the main idea of ¶5? _____

_____

9. What are the supporting details for ¶5? _____

_____

_____

6 | Understanding Demonstrative Pronouns

Write what each demonstrative pronoun refers to in the text.

1. These (These are able to stabilize estrogen) (¶2) _isoflavones_ _____

2. This (This was demonstrated) (¶4) _____

3. those (those whose diet didn't include isoflavones) (¶5) _____

4. These (These are compounds) (¶6) _____

5. These (These are all ready) (¶8) _____

VOCABULARY STRATEGY Understanding Vocabulary in Context—
Parallel Clauses

Parallel clauses are two clauses that occur next to each other—either in the same sentence or in two sentences that are next to each other. The clauses are *parallel* because they contain the same grammatical structure. Sometimes, parallel clauses can help a reader understand meaning by repeating, reinforcing, defining, or explaining information.

Read the following sentences.

Fortunately, there are now a variety of soy and tofu products that are both *convenient* and tasty. Both fresh and long-conservation soymilk are *easy to find* in many super-markets, and soymilk can be used in place of cow's milk for both drinking and cooking. (¶3)

The first clause uses *convenient* to describe soy and tofu products. The second clause reinforces this adjective by explaining again that soymilk products are *easy to find*. The grammatical structures of the two clauses are similar. Both *convenient* and *easy to find* are adjectives; they have a similar meaning.

7 | Understanding Vocabulary in Context

A. **Parallel Clauses.** Underline the word or phrase that means the same thing as the *italicized* word.

1. These are able to *stabilize* estrogen, a female hormone necessary for normal growth and development. They adjust the hormone's effects when levels are too high or low. (¶2)

2. This was *demonstrated* in an analysis of 38 studies published in the prestigious *New England Journal of Medicine*. The analysis showed that eating soy lowers total levels of cholesterol by 10% and LDL or "bad" cholesterol by 13%. (¶4)

3. Although both men and women are *susceptible*, women are especially at risk. (¶5)

B. **Context Clues.** Select the best meaning for each word and phrase according to the text.

1. to be on a par with (¶1)

    a. to be as good as   b. to be inferior to   c. to have problems with

2. to give (someone or something) the green light (¶4)

    a. to disagree with   b. to disapprove of   c. to give approval to

3. to revert to (¶6)

    a. to attack   b. to stop being   c. to return to

4. to prevent (¶6)

    a. to keep from happening   b. to make happen   c. to promote

5. to block (¶6)

    a. to destroy   b. to prevent   c. to assist

8 | Reading Critically—Facts, Opinions, and Inferences

Write *F* for *Fact*, *O* for *Opinion*, or *I* for *Inference* according to the text. Discuss your answers with a partner.

___O___ 1. Eating soy is one of the simplest things we can do to boost our health.

_____ 2. Whole foods like tofu, soymilk, and tempeh contain higher levels of isoflavones than supplements.

_____ 3. People who would like to lower their cholesterol could incorporate soy products into their diet.

_____ 4. Soy-based burgers, hot dogs, deli meats, and bacon have a taste and texture that is very similar to real meats.

_____ 5. Almost anyone who wants a better diet should eat more soy.

9 | Discussing the Issues

Answer the questions and discuss your answers with a partner.

1. Do you think foods such as tofu and soymilk are tasty? Why or why not?

2. Do you think people are influenced by reading studies on health benefits of foods like soy? Why or why not?

3. Do you find the medical studies on the benefits of soy convincing enough so that you will incorporate it into your diet? Why or why not?

Text 3 | Pyramids of Health

1 | Getting Started

Complete the chart and then briefly discuss your answers with a partner.

I eat . . .	Monthly	Weekly	Daily	Never
bread, rice, noodles, or pasta	☐	☐	☐	☐
eggs	☐	☐	☐	☐
fish or shellfish	☐	☐	☐	☐
fruits and vegetables	☐	☐	☐	☐
meat (beef, pork, lamb, etc.)	☐	☐	☐	☐
poultry (chicken, turkey, duck, goose, etc.)	☐	☐	☐	☐
sweets (candy, pastries, cakes, ice cream, etc.)	☐	☐	☐	☐

2 | Active Previewing

Preview the diagrams on the next page and then answer the questions with a partner.

1. What regions are represented by the diagrams?

2. What is the topic of these diagrams?

> **REMINDER**
>
> Preview diagrams by reading the title, the subtitles, and then by looking at the diagrams as a whole.
> For more on *previewing diagrams*, see page 130.

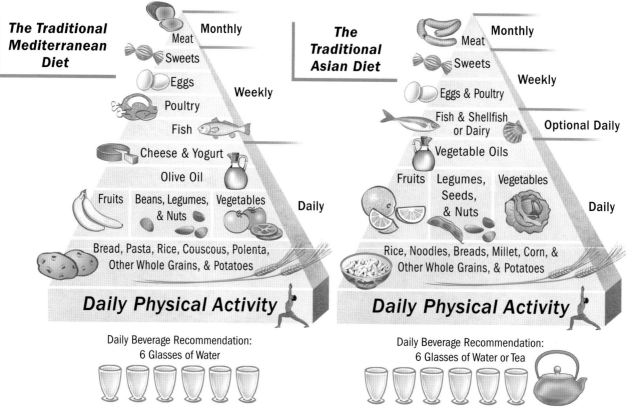

The Traditional Mediterranean Diet

Monthly
Meat

Weekly
Sweets
Eggs
Poultry
Fish

Daily
Cheese & Yogurt
Olive Oil
Fruits | Beans, Legumes, & Nuts | Vegetables
Bread, Pasta, Rice, Couscous, Polenta, Other Whole Grains, & Potatoes

Daily Physical Activity

Daily Beverage Recommendation:
6 Glasses of Water

The Traditional Asian Diet

Monthly
Meat

Weekly
Sweets
Eggs & Poultry

Optional Daily
Fish & Shellfish or Dairy

Daily
Vegetable Oils
Fruits | Legumes, Seeds, & Nuts | Vegetables
Rice, Noodles, Breads, Millet, Corn, & Other Whole Grains, & Potatoes

Daily Physical Activity

Daily Beverage Recommendation:
6 Glasses of Water or Tea

3 | Understanding the Graphics

Answer the questions according to the graphics. Discuss your answers with a partner.

1. Which foods are eaten the least often (in both diets)? _____

2. What is the recommendation for consuming sweets? _____

3. Which foods are eaten the most frequently (in both diets)? _____

4 | Reading Critically—Facts, Opinions, and Inferences

Write *F* for *Fact*, *O* for *Opinion*, or *I* for *Inference* according to the graphics. Discuss your answers with a partner.

___F___ 1. The Mediterranean diet pyramid recommends daily consumption of olive oil.

_____ 2. Fish is more healthful than meat.

_____ 3. The Asian diet pyramid recommends six glasses of water or tea per day.

_____ 4. Fruits should be eaten daily.

_____ 5. People who get daily physical activity have better health.

5 | Discussing the Issues

Answer the questions and discuss your answers with a partner.

1. Which pyramid represents the most healthful diet? Why?

2. What are the advantages and disadvantages of following the two diets in the food pyramids?

3. Draw a pyramid that resembles your diet. How is it similar to or different from the Mediterranean and Asian food pyramids?

Text 4 | Spice It Up

1 | Getting Started

A. Answer the questions and briefly discuss your answers with a partner.

1. Do you like spicy food?

2. Is there a lot of spicy food in your country?

3. How do you feel when you eat spicy food? Describe what happens.

4. What makes spicy food "hot"?

5. What health benefits do you think eating spicy food might have?

B. Complete the chart and then briefly discuss your answers with a partner.

Countries that have spicy cuisines
1.
2.
3.

2 | Skimming

Skim the online article on the next page in five minutes or less. Then answer the questions with a partner.

1. Are chili peppers a fruit or a vegetable?

2. What is capsicum?

3. Where were chili peppers first cultivated?

4. What are three places, regions, or countries mentioned in the article that use chili peppers in their cuisines?

5. What is one medical benefit offered by chili peppers?

B. Work as a class or in large groups. Try to name as many things as you can about the text.

C. Answer the questions with a partner.

1. What is the topic of this text?

2. What is the main idea of this text?

> **REMINDER**
> Skim the text by reading the title, the introduction, the first paragraph, the first sentence of each paragraph, the final paragraph of the text, and by looking at the photograph and the caption. Note names, places, and dates. For more on *skimming*, see page 149.

A. Read the text. Stop after each paragraph and tell a partner two things that you remember about it.

Chili Peppers and Globalization

by Jerry Hopkins

1 Chili peppers are decidedly an international phenomenon, spicing up regional dishes from Thailand to North Africa. In Thailand Confidential, this week's Globalist Bookshelf selection, Jerry Hopkins gives insight to the culture and history surrounding this fiery fruit (yes, technically a fruit) and highlights how it may be one of the world's best medical miracles.

There are many different kinds of chili peppers

2 In Thailand—where restaurants rate their dishes by placing one, two, three, and sometimes four little red chilis on the menu next to the dishes' names to alert diners—I am tolerated[1]. Barely.

3 A longtime friend, who is a Thai chef, used to bring home food purchased at street stalls and as she placed this on the table, she would point to one container and say, "Mine," then to another, saying, "Yours." As if to say, "Poor dear."

4 Thailand is not the birthplace of the Capsicum, or chili pepper; it only acts as if it is. In fact, the chili was imported, along with much else in the national diet. However, in Thailand the per capita consumption[2] of the small, fiery fruit is surely as high if not higher than it is anywhere else. And it is in the use of unprocessed, fresh, ripe chilis where Thailand rings all the loudest bells.

5 The truth is that chili is an international phenomenon. There is a bimonthly magazine published in the United States, Chile Pepper (there is no agreement on the spelling), and a wide variety of products is available, including pepper-shaped wind chimes, bells, and strings of Christmas tree lights. There is even a Hot Sauce Club of America; members receive two new hot sauces and a newsletter every month. There is even a popular American rock and roll band that calls itself the Red Hot Chili Peppers. Yes, the band is hot.

continued

---

[1] **to tolerate:** to endure (something or someone), even if one doesn't like or appreciate (it/him/her)

[2] **per capita consumption:** amount consumed per person within a specific population

6   Chilis are hot because they contain capsaicin (pronounced cap-SAY-a-sin), an irritant alkaloid found mostly in the interior tissue to which the seeds are attached. (Thus, removing the seeds helps lower the temperature.) Capsaicin has at least five separate chemical components. Three of these deliver an immediate kick to the throat at the back of the palate, and the two others convey a slower, longer lasting, and less fierce heat on the tongue and mid-palate. Mmm-mmmmmm-mmm, say my Thai friends, who have had decades to get used to it.

7   Chili peppers were first cultivated in Middle and South America. Christopher Columbus (Cristoforo Colombo) came upon them in the Caribbean and brought them back to Spain from his second voyage to the West Indies. The Portuguese explorer Fernando Magellan (Fernao de Magalhaes) is attributed with taking chili peppers to Africa, while other less famous Portuguese explorers are credited with taking them to Asia.

8   Belonging to the same family as the tomato and the eggplant (also technically fruits), today chili peppers play a significant role in many cuisines—from Mexican, where they are used in ragouts and sauces (moles), to Middle Eastern, where they are pickled whole, to North African, where they are used with garlic to season couscous, to South Indian, where they are an essential ingredient in curries.

9   There are widely varying ways of preparing the sauces and different uses for them from country to country. The Chinese make a purée, called ra-yiu, that is mostly oil-based and includes fried soy bean and chili as additional ingredients. In fact, so popular is chili in China that each province has its own brand.

10 In Korea, chili paste is used to make kimchee and hot spicy soup. In Singapore, chili sauce must include garlic and ginger, while in Malaysia and Indonesia, chili paste is called sambal and often includes shrimp or dried fish. In Hawaii, "chili peppa water"—which is a blend of what it sounds like—is found on every local restaurant table next to the pepper and salt.

11 Throughout the United States, chili pepper sauce has a large following, mainly through the sale of Tabasco® sauce. This is manufactured[3] in Louisiana, sold in tiny bottles internationally, and is used to season meat, egg, and red kidney bean dishes, sauces, and a number of cocktails, including the ever-fashionable Bloody Mary. Not long ago, for a year or so, chili sauce even outsold ketchup in the States.

12 Tabasco® tastes somewhat sourer and, in fact, is hotter than sauce in Thailand. It is fermented in barrels for three years or longer, while in Thailand, the major ingredients—chili, flour, and tomato paste—are merely blended together, and there is no fermentation involved. Thais, too, like their sauce free-flowing, whereas in other countries in Southeast Asia, the thicker and slower, the better.

continued

---

[3] **to manufacture:** to make; to produce

13 From a medical perspective, too, chili peppers are attracting attention. Not only does the consumption of a single pepper provide a full day's supply of beta-carotene and nearly twice the recommended daily allowance of Vitamin C for an adult, but also that same ingredient that makes chilis hot, capsaicin, controls pain and makes us feel better. "What's that? Makes me feel *better*?"

14 Consider what happens when you bite into a chili pepper. You think you have a volcano in your mouth, with explosions going off from lips to gums to tongue and throat. You're certain that your taste buds[4] have been defoliated; it's as if they've been stripped from your tongue. You break into a sweat and reach for your water glass to put out the fire. (A pointless exercise because capsaicin is barely soluble in water. The best thing is to drink milk because casein, one of the proteins in milk, specifically and directly counteracts the effects of capsaicin. Others swear by water mixed with a dash of salt.) Your eyes water and your nasal passages flood.

15 At the same time, there may come a strange relief, a beneficial side effect[5]. The messages sent to your brain are similar to those that mark pain, and the brain responds to these by stimulating the secretion of extra endorphins, natural hormones produced by the body that give pleasure. The production of the endorphins then soothes or reduces existing pain not only in the mouth, but also throughout the body.

16 So far, studies suggest capsaicin reduces pain associated with arthritis, diabetes, muscle and joint problems, cluster headaches, and phantom limbs. A study done at the famed Mayo Clinic in the United States further suggests that it reduces pain from post-surgical scars. Thus, many people who suffer from chronic pain are now being advised to eat spicy food, either as an alternative or as a supplement to analgesics. It is, then, quite literally, fighting fire with fire.

17 Chili peppers possess other medicinal advantages. They alleviate symptoms of the common cold by breaking up congestion and keeping the airways clear. (Did you notice that your nose and eyes started running when you broke out in that initial sweat? A capsaicin nose spray is now being considered to relieve headaches and migraines.) Chili peppers increase one's metabolic rate, contributing to the success of a weight-loss program. Furthermore, they also contain an anti-oxidant that lowers the "bad" cholesterol. And scientists at the famed Max Planck Institute in Germany confirm Capsicum can prevent the formation of blood clots by lengthening the time it takes blood to coagulate.

18 Only a short walk from my flat here in Thailand, there are street vendors mixing and selling som tam, a five-alarm green papaya salad with lime juice and tomato and as many chopped peppers as one can stand. This once was a staple for the poor in Thailand's impoverished northeast, but nowadays it's hard to find a Thai menu anywhere worldwide that doesn't include it.

continued

---

[4] **taste buds:** the tiny bumps on the tongue that allow us to experience the sense of taste

[5] **side effect:** a secondary effect of a drug or some kind of therapy

19 My Thai chef friend, who is reading over my shoulder as I write this, is calling me the Thai equivalent of wimp. She keeps a jar of dried seeds in my kitchen and casually dumps them into soups and onto noodle and rice dishes in a manner that seems suicidal.

20 "Getting to like chili peppers is like playing with fire," said Dr. Paul Rozin, a psychologist at the University of Pennsylvania in the United States. "Humans tend to put themselves voluntarily in situations which their body tells them to avoid—but humans tend to get pleasures out of these things, such as eating chili peppers or going on roller coaster rides. We are the only species that enjoys such things. No one has ever found an animal that likes to frighten itself."

B. Read the text again without pausing. Tell your partner two new things that you remember.

C. Work as a class or in large groups. Try to name as many things as you can about the text.

4 | Understanding the Text

A. Answer as many questions as you can without looking at the text. Discuss your answers with a partner.

1. How do Thai people feel about chili peppers? _____

2. What makes chili peppers spicy? _____

3. In what regions do people eat chili peppers? _____

4. What has one medical study shown about the effects of eating chilis? _____

_____

5. How does Dr. Paul Rozin explain people's liking for chili peppers? _____

_____

B. Complete the chart according to the text. Discuss your answers with a partner.

Condition	What chili peppers can do
1. pain	They can reduce pain by activating endorphins.
2. the common cold	
3. metabolic rate	
4. cholesterol	
5. blood clots	

5 | Understanding the Topic, Main Idea, and Supporting Details

A. **Text.** Answer the questions and discuss your answers with a partner.

1. What is the topic of the text? _____

2. What is the main idea of the text? _____

_____

_____

3. Are your answers for topic and main idea here the same as those you determined after you
   skimmed the text, or are your answers different? _____

B. **Paragraphs.** Answer the questions and discuss your answers with a partner.

1. What is the topic of ¶13? _____

2. What is the main idea of ¶13? _____

_____

3. What are the supporting details for ¶13? _____

_____

_____

4. What is the topic of ¶16? _____

5. What is the main idea of ¶16? _____

_____

6. What are the supporting details for ¶16? _____

_____

_____

7. What is the topic of ¶17? _____

8. What is the main idea of ¶17? _____

_____

9. What are the supporting details for ¶17? _____

_____

_____

_____

_____

6 | Understanding Demonstrative Pronouns

Write what each demonstrative pronoun refers to in the text.

1. this (this on the table) (¶3) _food purchased at street stalls_
2. these (three of these) (¶6) _____
3. This (This is manufactured) (¶11) _____
4. those (those that mark pain) (¶15) _____
5. This (This once was a staple food) (¶18) _____

7 | Understanding Vocabulary in Context

A. Parallel Clauses. Use parallel clauses to help you write the best meaning for each word or phrase according to the text.

1. to deliver (¶6) _____
2. to be attributed with (¶7) _____
3. to be defoliated (¶14) _____

B. Context Clues. Match each verb on the left with its definition on the right according to the text.

_____ 1. to cultivate (¶7)   a. to lessen the pain of something

_____ 2. to season (¶8, ¶11)   b. to endure; to accept

_____ 3. to ferment (¶12)   c. to add flavor to

_____ 4. to alleviate (¶17)   d. to grow

_____ 5. to stand (¶18)   e. to allow a (usually) liquid substance to age in order
                                            to create a chemical and flavor change

8 | Reading Critically—Facts, Opinions, and Inferences

Write F for *Fact*, O for *Opinion*, or I for *Inference* according to the text. Discuss your answers with a partner.

___F___ 1. The chili pepper is technically a fruit.

_____ 2. The writer doesn't like to eat very spicy food, but his friend does.

_____ 3. Chili peppers are an international phenomenon.

_____ 4. Many Koreans enjoy spicy food.

_____ 5. Studies suggest that capsaicin reduces arthritis pain.

9 | Discussing the Issues

Answer the questions and discuss your answers with a partner.

1. Do you think it is strange to love extremely spicy food? Why or why not?

2. Do you think this text could persuade someone to eat more chili peppers? Why or why not?

3. According to Dr. Paul Rozin (¶20) people's liking for chili peppers is due to their getting pleasure from frightening themselves. Do you agree with this analysis? Why or why not?

Putting It On Paper

A. Write a five-paragraph essay on one of these topics.

1. A friend or relative wants to improve his or her diet for health reasons and asks you to help create a gradual plan for more healthful nutrition. Describe the process you will recommend.

2. Describe how a food, a food product, or a food style—such as vegetarianism or fast food—might gradually become popular.

Steps for your essay

a. In your first paragraph, clearly state your recommendation or opinion about your topic and your general reason or reasons why.

b. Your second, third, and fourth paragraphs should each contain a different reason that supports your topic.

c. In your final paragraph, summarize the ideas you state in your essay.

B. Exchange essays with a partner. First, read your partner's essay and answer the questions on the checklist. Then give feedback to your partner.

> **NOTE**
> Each of your paragraphs should contain a main idea that is supported by details—facts, data, examples, etc.—that prove or illustrate your main idea. For more on *supporting details*, see page 77.

✔ CHECKLIST

1. Does ¶1 show your partner's recommendation or opinion about the topic?
2. Do the three body paragraphs support the topic?
3. Does the final paragraph summarize the ideas contained in the essay?
4. Does each paragraph contain a main idea?
5. Do the details of each paragraph support the main idea?
6. Are you persuaded by your partner's recommendation or opinion?
7. Is there any information in the essay that is not related to your partner's thesis? If yes, please underline it on your partner's essay, and write it below:

_____

_____

_____

_____

_____

C. Revise your work based on your partner's feedback.

Taking It Online | Food and More Food

A. With a partner, use the Internet to research healthful and unhealthful foods.

1. Use Google (www.google.com) or another major search engine to begin your online research.

2. Search for websites with information about two foods that are believed to be good for long-term health and two foods that aren't. In addition to the food name, these words may be helpful in your search:

   food

   health benefit

   health risk

   beneficial

   damaging

   healthful

3. Preview the websites.

ONLINE TIP

Many large websites have their own search engines. Use these search engines to help save time when looking for information related to your search.

B. Complete the table with the information you find.

Healthful Foods	
Food:	Food:
Website:	Website:
Benefit:	Benefit:

Unhealthful Foods	
Food:	Food:
Website:	Website:
Benefit:	Benefit:

C. Following up. In small groups, discuss your eating habits. Think of three ways you could use the information you found on the Internet to improve your own diet.

Chapter 8

Ethics in Science

Answer the questions and briefly discuss your answers with a partner.

1. Do you think medical research is important?

2. Look at the photos. What kind of medical research could be involved in each of these situations?

3. What are some of the advantages and disadvantages of medical research?

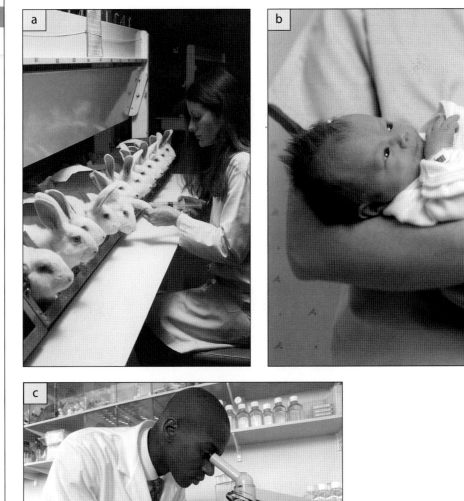

Text 1 | Should Animals Have Rights?

1 | Getting Started

A. Check the products that you consume and the products that you think are tested on animals. Then answer the question that follows. Briefly discuss your answers with a partner.

Products	I Consume	Tested on animals
1. cosmetics (such as make-up, lotions, and creams)	☐	☐
2. deodorant	☐	☐
3. CDs	☐	☐
4. hairspray	☐	☐
5. household cleaning products	☐	☐
6. medicine for colds and flu	☐	☐
7. digital cameras	☐	☐
8. shampoo and toothpaste	☐	☐

Do you think animal testing is necessary to ensure the safety of the products you checked?

B. Answer the questions on the next page and briefly discuss your answers with a partner.

a

a horse

b

a rabbit

c

a dog

d

a mouse

e

a pig

f

a cat

g

a cow

h

a sheep

1. Look at the photos. Which animals are used for testing?

2. Do you think any of these animals should not be used for testing? Why or why not?

3. Should there be laws or criteria regarding the living conditions for animals that are used in laboratory experiments? Why or why not?

2 | Active Previewing

A. Preview the newspaper article below by reading the first two paragraphs. Then discuss your answers with a partner.

1. **Which university** and **which group** are discussed in this article?

2. **What** is problematic?

3. **When** did the group make their statement?

4. **Where** does the testing take place?

B. Work as a class or in large groups. Try to name as many things as you can about the text.

C. Then answer these questions with a partner.

1. What is the topic of this text?

2. What is the main idea of this text?

3 | Reading and Recalling

A. Read the text. Stop after each subtitled section and tell a partner two things that you remember about it.

Rutgers Continues Animal Testing Despite Activists' Concerns

BY JESSICA ANSERT

1 **Universities' Tests Raise Concerns**

Needless to say, as a research institution, Rutgers University conducts plenty of research. The University's animal research involves a wide range of animals, from rodents—such as mice and rats—to horses, and uses the research for advances in husbandry[1] and biomedicine.

2 While this is a straightforward issue for most people, groups such as People for the Ethical Treatment of Animals (PETA) recently said the University's testing of animals for research is problematic.

3 PETA has targeted other schools, as well, such as Columbia University, the University of Wisconsin, and Johns Hopkins University for what the group believes to be cruel practices in animal research.

continued

---

[1] **husbandry:** the application of scientific principals to animal breeding

continued

4 Valuable Results

University researchers said that although testing on animals is rarely the first choice, it leads to valuable results.

5 New advances include nervous system re-growth for spinal cord injuries and the development of better nutrition for horses, which has led to fewer bone development problems, said Larry Katz, chair of the department of animal science.

6 Despite the advances, Ben Peterson, a youth activist liaison[2] for PETA, believes that animal testing is not the only way to conduct such research.

7 "Certainly some medical developments were discovered through cruel animal tests," Peterson said. "But just because animals were used doesn't mean they were required."

8 Alternative Methods

PETA lists methods of research that don't require animal testing. The group's guidelines state, "Effective, affordable, and humane research methods include studies of human populations, volunteers and patients, as well as sophisticated in vitro[3], genomic[4], and computer-modeling techniques."

9 Katz said the University uses all of those techniques, in conjunction with[5] its research on animals. He emphasized that testing is done on animals when "it is the only way to answer the questions we are researching."

10 Systems for Limiting Cruelty

According to Katz, Rutgers has systems in place to limit the chances of cruel practices.

11 In 1994, the University adopted an Animal Welfare Policy to comply with Federal regulations, and it created a review board with a subcommittee to monitor the use of animals in research.

12 Michael J. Fennell, the director of the Animal Care Program at the University, said the committee ensures the rules are followed strictly rather than leniently.

13 "There are 15 to 16 members on the Animal Care and Facility Committee (ACFC) that go over every possible detail to make sure the animals are treated properly," Fennell said.

14 The ACFC has supervisors for different categories of animals—the equines, such as horses and mules; bovines, such as cows and oxen; pigs, sheep and goats, and deer; and laboratory animals, such as mice and rats.

15 The committee must inspect all of the University's animal facilities at least every six months. It also handles all complaints, which are dealt with confidentially.

16 The Animal Care program is also affiliated with federal licensing. According to its website, "The program works in conjunction with the University Office of Laboratory Animal Services and is registered with the United States Department of Agriculture and adheres to the regulations set forth in the Animal Welfare Act."

17 PETA points out, however, that the federal guidelines don't protect rats, mice, or birds, and according to PETA, they "make up 95 percent of the animals used in research."

18 Following the Rules

Katz responded this does not mean the University is abusing the animals not protected by the legislation.

19 "Not only do we have to follow the Federal AWA guidelines, we follow the public health service policy which includes all vertebrates, rats, mice, and birds," Katz said.

20 Katz pointed out that if the University is found to be violating the policy instead of obeying it, it could lose all federal funds.

21 Ongoing Debate

Whether or not the University should use animals in testing is an ongoing debate centered on the argument that the costs outweigh the benefits and vice versa.

22 Katz believes that the benefits of animal research outweigh the cost. "It is our obligation to take care of these animals and limit suffering," he said, "[but] animals deserve our protection, not rights."

23 Peterson said PETA's position puts more value in the animals, not the results. In a prepared statement, he quoted George Bernard Shaw to explain his position: "You do not settle whether an experiment is justified or not by merely showing it is of some use. The distinction is not between useful and useless experiments, but between barbarous and civilized behavior."

---

[2] **liaison:** a person who serves as a link between two groups or organizations

[3] **in vitro:** in an artificial environment, such as a test tube; literally, "in glass"

[4] **genomic:** the study of genes and their functions

[5] **in conjunction with:** together with

B. Read the text again without pausing. Tell your partner two new things that you remember.

C. Work as a class or in large groups. Try to name as many things as you can about the text.

4 | Understanding the Text

A. Answer as many questions as you can without looking at the text. Discuss your answers with a partner.

1. What kind of research is discussed in this article? _____

2. What kind of group is PETA? _____

3. What is PETA's main complaint about Rutgers University's research? _____
_____

B. Complete the chart according to the text. Discuss your answers with a partner.

Position on animal testing	
1. Larry Katz:	
2. Ben Peterson:	
3. Animal Care Program:	

5 | Understanding the Topic and Main Idea

Text. Answer the questions and discuss your answers with a partner.

1. What is the topic of the text? _____

2. What is the main idea of the text? _____
_____

3. Are your answers for the topic and main idea here the same as those you determined after you previewed the text, or are your answers different? _____

6 | Understanding Pronouns

Write what each pronoun refers to according to the text.

1. this (this is a straightforward issue) (¶1, ¶2) <u>that the University conducts</u>
   <u>research on animals</u>

2. It (It also handles) (¶15) _____

3. it (obeying it) (¶20) _____

4. he (he said) (¶22) _____

5. it (it is of some use) (¶23) _____

7 | Understanding Vocabulary in Context

A. Contrasts. Write the contrast for each word according to the text.

1. straightforward (¶2) <u>problematic</u>

2. leniently (¶12) _____

3. to obey (¶20) _____

B. Examples. Use examples to help you write a definition for each word according to the text.

1. rodents (¶1) <u>mice and rats</u>

2. equines (¶14) _____

3. bovines (¶14) _____

8 | Reading Critically—Facts, Opinions, and Inferences

Write F for Fact, O for Opinion, or I for Inference according to the text. Discuss your answers with a partner.

__O__ 1. The University's research on animals leads to valuable results.

_____ 2. PETA lists methods of research that don't require animal testing.

_____ 3. Some people who make complaints prefer to remain anonymous.

_____ 4. The University wants to keep its federal funding.

_____ 5. The benefits of animal research outweigh the costs.

9 | Discussing the Issues

Answer the questions and discuss your answers with a partner.

1. Do research advances justify the use of animal testing?

2. Do you think there is a need for a group like PETA? Why or why not?

3. How does the quotation from George Bernard Shaw (¶23) relate to animal testing?

Text 2 | Part Animal, Part Human?

1 | Getting Started

A. Answer the questions and briefly discuss your answers with a partner.

1. The mule in the photo on the right is a *hybrid* of which two animals?

    a. a zebra and a horse

    b. a horse and a donkey

    c. a donkey and a zebra

2. What are some other animal hybrids?

3. Why might scientists or biologists create hybrids?

B. Circle the number that expresses how much you agree or disagree with each statement. Briefly discuss your answers with a partner.

1. It is okay to cross two species of animals, such as a horse and a donkey, for work or medical purposes.

Strongly Disagree		Neutral		Strongly Agree
1	2	3	4	5

2. It is okay for scientists to cross human cells with animal cells for medical research purposes.

Strongly Disagree		Neutral		Strongly Agree
1	2	3	4	5

3. Any medical research that can help save human lives should be permitted.

Strongly Disagree		Neutral		Strongly Agree
1	2	3	4	5

2 | Active Previewing

A. Preview the online article on the next page and tell a partner two things you remember about it.

B. Work as a class or in large groups. Try to name as many things as you can about the text.

C. Answer the questions with a partner.

1. What is the topic of this text?

2. What is the main idea of this text?

A. Read the text. Stop after each paragraph and tell a partner two things that you remember about it.

Animal-Human Hybrids Spark Controversy

by Maryann Mott

1 **The First Hybrids**
Scientists have begun blurring the line between human and animal by producing chimeras—hybrid creatures that are part human, part animal.

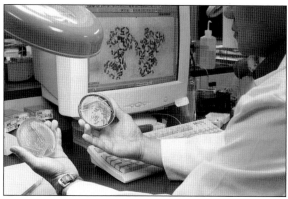

A researcher working in a laboratory

2 Chinese scientists at the Shanghai Second Medical University in 2003 successfully fused human cells with rabbit eggs. After the cells and eggs were successfully joined, the embryos were allowed to develop for several days in a laboratory dish before the scientists destroyed the embryos to harvest their stem cells[1].

3 In Minnesota in 2004 researchers at the Mayo Clinic created pigs with human blood flowing through their bodies. And at Stanford University in California an experiment might be done to create mice with human brains.

4 Scientists feel that more humanlike animals make better research models for testing drugs or possibly for growing "spare parts," such as livers, to transplant into humans. Watching how human cells mature and interact in a living creature may also lead to the discoveries of new medical treatments

5 But creating human-animal chimeras—creatures named after a monster in Greek mythology that had a lion's head, goat's body, and serpent's tail—has raised troubling questions: What new subhuman combination should be produced and for what purpose? At what point would it be considered human? And what rights, if any, should it have?

6 **Ethical Guidelines**
The United States currently has no federal laws that address these issues. The National Academy of Sciences, which advises the U.S. government, has been studying the issue. In March it plans to present voluntary ethical guidelines for researchers.

continued

---

[1] **stem cell:** a cell that can transform into and generate many other kinds of cells

continued

7. Biotechnology activist Jeremy Rifkin is opposed to crossing species because he believes animals have the right to exist without being tampered with or crossed with another species. "One doesn't have to be…into animal rights to think this doesn't make sense," he said. "It's the scientists who want to do this. They've now gone over the edge into the pathological domain[2]."

8. **Human Born to Mice Parents?**
David Magnus, director of the Stanford Center for Biomedical Ethics at Stanford University, believes the real worry is whether or not chimeras will be put to uses that are problematic, risky, or dangerous. For example, an experiment that would raise concerns, he said, is genetically engineering mice to produce human sperm and eggs, then doing in vitro fertilization to produce a child whose parents are a pair of mice. "Most people would find that problematic," Magnus said, "but those uses are bizarre and not, to the best of my knowledge, anything that anybody is remotely contemplating[3]. Most uses of chimeras are actually much more relevant to practical concerns."

9. In 2004, Canada passed the Assisted Human Reproduction Act, which bans chimeras. Specifically, it prohibits transferring a nonhuman cell into a human embryo and putting human cells into a nonhuman embryo.

10. Irv Weissman, director of Stanford University's Institute of Cancer/Stem Cell Biology and Medicine in California, is against a ban in the United States. Weissman feels that people shouldn't put their own moral beliefs in the way of this kind of science. "If that leads to a ban or moratorium[4]…they are stopping research that would save human lives," he said.

11. **Mice With Human Brains**
Weissman has already created mice with brains that are about one percent human. Soon he may conduct another experiment in which the mice have 100 percent human brains. This would be done, he said, by injecting human neurons (nerve cells) into the brains of embryonic mice. Before being born, the mice would be killed and dissected, or cut apart, to see if the architecture of a human brain had formed. If the overall structure had formed, he'd look for traces, or signs, of human cognitive[5] behavior.

12. Weissman said he's not a mad scientist trying to create a human in an animal body. He hopes the experiment leads to a better understanding of how the brain works, which would be useful in treating diseases like Alzheimer's or Parkinson's. The test has not yet begun, as he is waiting to read the National Academy's report, due out in a few months.

continued

---

[2] **pathological domain:** a mentally unstable area; an unnatural and destructive area

[3] **to contemplate:** to think about; to consider

[4] **moratorium:** suspension; halt; pause

[5] **cognitive:** refers to a mental process of reasoning, memory, judgment, and comprehension

continued

13 William Cheshire, associate professor of neurology at the Mayo Clinic's Jacksonville, Florida, branch feels that combining human and animal neurons is problematic. "This is unexplored biologic territory," he said. He believes that even if limits were set for such experimentation, there would be a significant risk of exceeding that limit before it could be recognized.

14 Cheshire supports research that combines human and animal cells to study cellular function. But where he draws the ethical line is on research that would create an organism that is partly human and partly animal.

B. Read the text again without pausing. Tell your partner two new things that you remember.

C. Work as a class or in large groups. Try to name as many things as you can about the text.

4 | Understanding the Text

A. Answer as many questions as you can without looking at the text. Discuss your answers with a partner.

1. What are chimeras? _____

2. What is the main reason for creating chimeras? _____

3. What is the biggest ethical issue with regard to creating chimeras? _____

_____

B. Complete the chart according to the text. Discuss your answers with a partner.

Scientific Experiments	has happened already	has not happened (yet)
1. Scientists fuse human cells with rabbit eggs.	✔	☐
2. Researchers create pigs with human blood.	☐	☐
3. Mice are genetically engineered to produce human sperm and eggs.	☐	☐
4. Scientist creates mice with brains that are one percent human.	☐	☐
5. Scientist creates mice with brains that are 100% human.	☐	☐

5 | Understanding the Topic and Main Idea

Text. Answer the questions and discuss your answers with a partner.

1. What is the topic of the text? _____

_____

2. What is the main idea of the text? _____

_____

_____

3. Are your answers for the topic and main idea here the same as those you determined after you previewed the text, or are your answers different? _____

6 | Understanding Demonstrative Pronouns

Write what each demonstrative pronoun refers to according to the text.

1. this (this doesn't make sense) (¶7) _tampering with or crossing species_

2. this (the scientists who want to do this) (¶7) _____

3. that (would find that problematic) (¶8) _____

4. that (that leads to a ban) (¶10) _____

5. this (This would be done) (¶11) _____

7 | Understanding Vocabulary in Context

A. Synonyms. Write the synonym for each word according to the text.

1. chimeras (¶1) _hybrid creatures that are part human, part animal_

2. to dissect (¶11) _____

3. traces (¶11) _____

B. Parallel Clauses. Use parallel clauses to help you write the definition of each word according to the text.

1. to fuse (¶2) _to join_ _____

2. to ban (¶9) _____

3. architecture (¶11) _____

8 | Reading Critically—Facts, Opinions, and Inferences

Write *F* for *Fact*, *O* for *Opinion*, or *I* for *Inference* according to the text. Discuss your answers with a partner.

___F___ 1. Chimeras are hybrids that are part human and part animal.

_____ 2. Watching how human cells mature and interact may lead to the discoveries of new medical treatments.

_____ 3. The National Academy of Sciences believes that researchers need to follow ethical guidelines.

_____ 4. David Magnus is the director of the Stanford Center for Biomedical Ethics at Stanford University.

_____ 5. It is unethical to make human-animal hybrids.

9 | Discussing the Issues

Answer the questions and discuss your answers with a partner.

1. Do you believe that research involving chimeras should be allowed, partly allowed, or illegal? Why?

2. Do you think governments should impose strict limits on what researchers can or cannot do with regard to chimeras? If so, what? If not, why not?

3. At what point do you think a chimera should be considered human? What rights, if any, should it have?

Text 3 | Public Opinion on Gene Therapy

1 | Getting Started

Circle the number that expresses how much you approve or disapprove of each statement. Briefly discuss your answers with a partner.

1. modifying genes for the purpose of eliminating blindness or deafness

Strongly Disapprove		Neutral		Strongly Approve
1	2	3	4	5

2. modifying genes for the purpose of eliminating disease

Strongly Disapprove		Neutral		Strongly Approve
1	2	3	4	5

3. modifying genes to improve intelligence

Strongly Disapprove		Neutral		Strongly Approve
1	2	3	4	5

4. modifying genes to alter height or weight

Strongly Disapprove		Neutral		Strongly Approve
1	2	3	4	5

2 | Active Previewing

Preview the graphs below and then answer the questions with a partner.

1. What are the four potential areas of gene therapy use assessed in the graphs?

2. What is the topic of the graphs?

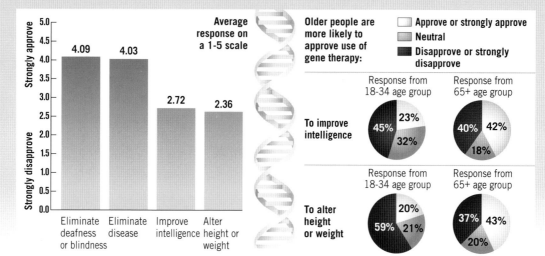

High Hopes for Gene Therapy

Eventually, doctors may be able to modify genes for all kinds of reasons. How do you feel about using gene therapy for each of the following?

Average response on a 1-5 scale

Older people are more likely to approve use of gene therapy:

- ☐ Approve or strongly approve
- ▨ Neutral
- ■ Disapprove or strongly disapprove

Bar chart (Strongly disapprove 0.0 to Strongly approve 5.0):
- Eliminate deafness or blindness: 4.09
- Eliminate disease: 4.03
- Improve intelligence: 2.72
- Alter height or weight: 2.36

To improve intelligence
- Response from 18-34 age group: 45%, 23%, 32%
- Response from 65+ age group: 40%, 42%, 18%

To alter height or weight
- Response from 18-34 age group: 59%, 20%, 21%
- Response from 65+ age group: 37%, 43%, 20%

3 | Scanning

Scan the table for the answers to the questions in three minutes or less. Discuss your answers with a partner.

1. What was the average response for using gene therapy to alter height or weight? _____

2. What was the average response for using gene therapy to eliminate disease? _____

3. Which use of gene therapy has the lowest average approval rating? _____

4. What percentage of 18-34 year-olds approve of using gene therapy to improve intelligence? _____

5. Are people 65+ years old more likely to approve the use of gene therapy to improve intelligence or approve it to alter height and weight? _____

4 | Making Inferences

Make two more inferences with a partner according to the graphics.

1. _Younger adults value intelligence more than height and weight._

2. _____

3. _____

5 | Discussing the Issues

Answer the questions and discuss your answers with a partner.

1. Why do you think older people seem to approve the use of gene therapy more than younger people do?

2. How do you feel about the use of gene therapy to improve intelligence? To alter height or weight?

3. For what other reasons, if any, might you approve of the use of gene therapy? Why? (If your answer is "none," why?)

Text 4 | Savior Siblings, Designer Babies

1 | Getting Started

A. Answer the questions and briefly discuss your answers with a partner.

1. Do you know any families in which people strongly resemble each other?

2. Check (✔) all of the characteristics that we inherit from the genes of our biological parents.

☐ a. hair and eye color

☐ b. the health of our teeth

☐ c. taste in fashion

☐ d. music preferences

☐ e. the shape of our face

☐ f. height

☐ g. the likelihood of getting certain diseases

☐ h. food preference

3. If you were given the opportunity to choose what your baby would look like, would you take the opportunity? Why or why not?

B. Answer the questions and briefly discuss your answers with a partner.

1. Check (✔) all of the medical procedures that you think are possible with today's medical technology.

☐ a. discovering if an unborn baby is male or female

☐ b. testing an unborn baby for certain diseases

☐ c. genetically changing certain characteristics of an unborn baby

☐ d. changing a person's genes to cure a disease

☐ e. preventing a genetically inherited disease from ever developing

2. Think of two genetic diseases, disorders, or problems you have heard of, and write them here:

_____

_____

3. Is there any way to prevent these genetic diseases, disorders, or problems?

2 | Skimming

A. Skim the magazine article below in five minutes or less. Then answer the questions with a partner.

1. What did the Hashmis want to do?

2. What kind of a change could germline gene therapy bring?

3. How many species of humans could there be by the end of the third millennium?

> **REMEMBER**
>
> Skim the text by reading the title, the first paragraph, the first sentence of each paragraph, and the final paragraph of the text. Note names, places, dates, and numbers. There is no need for a separate preview.
> For more on *skimming*, see page 149.

B. Work as a class or in large groups. Try to name as many things as you can about the text.

C. Then answer these questions with a partner.

1. What is the topic of this text?

2. What is the main idea of this text?

3 | Reading and Recalling

A. Read the text. Stop after each subtitled section and tell a partner two things that you remember about it.

Science and Technology: Creating the Stuff of Life

by Steve Connor

1   The unhappy case of the Hashmi family reopened the debate over what is meant by "designer babies." Raj and Shahana Hashmi wanted to have a baby by in vitro fertilization (IVF), a method in which the egg is fertilized outside the woman's body. Not only did they want the baby to be free of genetic disease; they also wanted it to be tested so that it would match the tissue of their six-year-old son Zain, who was born with a rare blood disorder.

2   The Hashmis hoped that a "savior sibling" would save Zain's life. Their case was brought before the House of Lords, one of the houses of Great Britain's parliament, and they were granted permission to go ahead with their plan.

3   The term "designer baby" can describe a range of difficult issues that surround developments in reproductive medicine. Doctors are able to do "prenatal[1] genetic diagnosis" (PGD) by removing a single cell from an early IVF embryo and by genetically analyzing it. This enables them to test for a range of inherited disorders, as well as to carry out tissue analysis.

4   A "savior sibling," on the other hand, refers specifically to a child who is conceived to save the life of a brother or sister who suffers from a disease or other disorder by offering healthy genes. These children are tested while they are still embryos in order to ensure that they are free from genetic disorders.

5   **The Case of the Nashes**
    In 2000, Lisa and Jack Nash of Denver, Colorado were the first couple to benefit from the idea of creating a savior sibling by PGD when they decided to have their son, Adam. The Nashes are both "carriers" of Fanconi anemia, a rare inherited bone-marrow disease. Carriers do not have any symptoms of the disease themselves, but they have genes that are capable of passing the disease on to any children.

6   The Nashes had a daughter, Molly, who is now six, and who was in fact born with the disease. Scientists tested 15 of the Nashes' embryos for the presence of the diseased gene. They then went a step further to see which one also had the same tissue type as Molly. The result was Adam, who donated a stem-cell transplant[2] that helped his sister to recover.

7   For some, the idea of creating a baby to order is evil; for others, it is nothing more sinister than planning a family with the benefits of modern medicine. However, the complexities of the ethical and legal arguments over designer

---

[1] **prenatal:** before birth

[2] **stem-cell transplant:** a transfer from one body to another of unspecialized cells that can be made into specialized cells

continued

babies such as Adam will seem relatively unimportant compared to the intricacies of the debate that threatens to occur over the likely technological developments in reproductive genetics.

8 **Germline Gene Therapy: A Permanent Change?**

We are, to some extent, already accustomed to the idea of playing around with genes. Recently, doctors in London said they had successfully cured a second child of a fatal genetic condition with the help of gene therapy. The technique was able to transform the deadly gene into a normal, healthy version.

9 There are two kinds of gene therapy. Standard gene therapy targets only the tissues damaged by the faulty gene. Germline gene therapy involves redesigning genes at the stage of the embryo so that each and every cell of the resulting baby carries the newly inserted gene. This more extreme modification would have far-reaching consequences because it would also include changing the sperm and eggs of the mature adults. This would mean that the children of these adults would also inherit the altered genes. Therefore, potentially, germline gene therapy has the power of changing the genetic make-up of the human species for good.

10 Standard gene therapy in its early stages has had mixed results. Some early experiments led to some terrible outcomes. One of the most terrible was the case of Jesse Gelsinger, who died in 1999 after undergoing gene therapy that involved infecting him with a genetically engineered virus. The harmless virus was supposed to carry healthy genes to his liver. Instead, he suffered liver failure.

11 **Human Artificial Chromosomes**

In Britain, germline gene therapy is not allowed under current laws, but there may soon be calls to reexamine them, especially considering recent work into human artificial chromosomes (HACs). Humans have 46

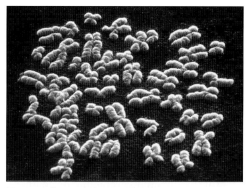
Human chromosomes at x2,100

chromosomes, and they store and transmit[3] all our genetic information. The idea behind the work on HACs is to add an extra chromosome, which would be called "cousin 47," or the 47th human chromosome. Some scientists believe that many of the safety concerns about germline gene therapy can be addressed by refining the technology that revolves around the 47th chromosome itself.

12 Supporters of this type of therapy say HACs are inherently safer than other ways of introducing foreign genes into the body. The reason for this is that the DNA of the artificial chromosomes is protected; it is enclosed in a structure, just as human DNA is naturally stored in each of our 46 chromosomes. Those who support this therapy believe HACs can be made to replicate, or copy themselves, reliably each time cells divide. Furthermore, it could be possible to turn these genes "on" or "off" at will. It might also be possible to include a self-destruct mechanism that would prevent the HAC from being passed on to future generations if this were a concern.

13 **When, How, and to What Extent?**

The neurobiologists Gregory Stock and John Campbell of the University of California at Los Angeles are among the leaders who promote the idea of using HACs for human germline gene therapy. They say it is easy to "pretend that human manipulations[4] can be ignored" in general discussions about genetic technology, but that realistically these manipulations will

continued

---

[3] **to transmit:** to pass down from parent to child; to convey

[4] **manipulation:** change or influence exerted on something

continued

occur. "The real question is not whether they will be applied to humans, but when, how, and to what extent."

14   Artificial chromosomes have been used in genetics for years. Huntington Willard of the Case Research University School of Medicine in Cleveland, Ohio made the first artificial human chromosome in 1997. He put three types of DNA in a test tube, and the primitive "chromosome" self-assembled. It survived in the cells for six months, apparently retaining its characteristics during cell division.

15   Chromosomes are complex structures, but there seem to be three crucial components necessary for them to replicate each time the cell divides. One is the *centromere*, a structure at the center of the chromosome that plays an essential role in cell division. Then there are the *telomeres* at the end of the chromosome (like the plastic tips of shoelaces that prevent them from unraveling). And finally there are the so-called origins of replication, the DNA *sequences* that initiate duplication of the chromosome during cell division.

16   Stock and Campbell believe it will soon be possible to consider truly radical therapies. These extreme treatments would involve inserting specially designed HACs into human embryos. Stock and Campbell say, for example, that it could be possible to create an HAC that could get rid of disease. An HAC with genes that would eliminate the risk of acquiring certain diseases could be placed directly in the embryo. Another idea is to introduce an HAC that contains a series of genetic "switches." These switches, when turned on, would trigger the destruction of diseased cells.

17   **A Gene Cassette and the Future**

If preventive treatments such as these are shown to work safely, it is not difficult to envision an array of treatments delivered as a "gene cassette" on a single HAC, just as a musical cassette has a number of songs. For example, per-

haps anti-aging genes could be added to every embryo's extra chromosome.

18   Stock and Campbell say, "Two things will be necessary before human germline engineering can occur broadly: a safe, reliable way of delivering genetic changes to a human embryo and genetic modifications so compelling that large numbers of parents will want them." They argue that both are nearer than many people believe because of recent developments in human artificial chromosomes. "The time to examine and discuss the realistic benefits and challenges these new reproductive technologies embody is now, while they are still nascent[5]. And to keep such discussion focused on realistic possibilities rather than science fiction, it is imperative that active researchers in the field participate," they say.

19   If germline gene therapy goes ahead, it is possible that human society could become divided between the "gene enriched," or GenRich humans, and the "naturals." Those who could afford the benefits the technology offers would improve their own lives and those of their children with gene enhancement, while those people could not afford to benefit from the technology would be left to live and procreate naturally. Since the resulting children would have no genetic modifications, this could result in two species of humans. Princeton University's Lee Silver believes that although such a frightening world is not in danger of happening in the immediate future, it is nonetheless plausible.

20   "If the accumulation of genetic knowledge and advances in genetic enhancement technology continue at the present rate," Silver says, "then by the end of the third millennium, the gene-enriched class and the natural class will become the GenRich humans and the Natural humans—entirely separate species with no ability to cross-breed and with as much romantic interest in each other as a current human would have for a chimpanzee."

---

[5] **nascent:** emerging; just coming into existence

B. Read the text again without pausing. Tell your partner two new things that you remember.

C. Work as a class or in large groups. Try to name as many things as you can about the text.

4 | Understanding the Text

A. Answer as many questions as you can without looking at the text. Discuss your answers with a partner.

1. What basic problem did the Hashmi family and the Nash family have in common?

   _____

   _____

2. What is a savior sibling? _____

   _____

   _____

3. What would be the purpose of a 47th chromosome? _____

   _____

   _____

4. What is a gene cassette? _____

   _____

   _____

5. According to Lee Silver, in what way would humans be different from the way they are now by the end of the third millennium? _____

   _____

   _____

B. Complete the chart according to the text. Discuss your answers with a partner.

The procedure or development	Standard therapy	"Germline" therapy
1. Tissues with a faulty gene can be repaired.	☐	☐
2. Genes are redesigned at the stage of the embryo.	☐	☐
3. Children inherit the altered genes of their parents.	☐	☐
4. A genetically modified virus was supposed to carry healthy genes to a man's liver.	☐	☐
5. Humans may receive genetic therapy through a 47th chromosome called "cousin 47."	☐	☐

5 | Understanding the Topic, Main Idea, and Supporting Details

A. Text. Answer the questions and discuss your answers with a partner.

1. What is the topic of the text? _____

2. What is the main idea of the text? _____

_____

_____

3. Are your answers for the topic and the main idea here the same as the ones you determined after you skimmed the text, or are your answers different? _____

B. Paragraphs. Answer the questions and discuss your answers with a partner.

1. What is the topic of ¶1? _____

2. What is the main idea of ¶1? _____

_____

3. What are the supporting details for ¶1? _____

_____

4. What is the topic of ¶4? _____

5. What is the main idea of ¶4? _____

_____

6. What are the supporting details for ¶4? _____

_____

7. What is the topic of ¶8? _____

8. What is the main idea of ¶8? _____

_____

9. What are the supporting details for ¶8? _____

_____

_____

_____

6 | Understanding Pronouns and Possessive Adjectives

Write what each pronoun or possessive adjective refers to according to the text.

1. (¶1)

   a. they (Not only did they want) _Raj and Shashana Hashmi_____

   b. they (they also wanted) _____

   c. it (they also wanted it) _____

   d. it (so that it would match) _____

   e. their (their six-year-old son) _____

2. (¶10)

    a. its (in its early stages) _____

    b. him (infecting him) _____

    c. his (his liver) _____

    d. he (he suffered) _____

3. (¶12)

    a. this (The reason for this) _____

    b. it (it is enclosed) _____

    c. themselves (copy themselves) _____

    d. it (it could be possible) _____

7 | Understanding Vocabulary in Context

A. Context Clues. Use context clues to help you write a definition for each word according to the text.

1. carrier (¶5) _a person who has genes that are capable of passing on a disease but who does not have any symptoms of the disease_

2. fatal (¶8) _____

3. to engineer (¶10) _____

4. to replicate (¶12) _____

5. radical (¶16) _____

6. to eliminate (¶16) _____

7. array (¶17) _____

8. to procreate (¶19) _____

B. Parallel Clauses. Use parallel clauses to help you write the definition of each word according to the text.

1. sinister (¶7) _evil_

2. intricacies (¶7) _____

3. to be enclosed (¶12) _____

8 | Reading Critically—Facts, Opinions, and Inferences

Write facts, opinions, and inferences according to the text.

1. Write one fact, one opinion, and one inference for ¶1.

Fact: _In vitro fertilization is a method in which the egg is fertilized outside_
the woman's body.

Opinion: _The case of the Hashmi family is an unhappy one._

Inference: _The Hashmis want to save the life of their son, Zain._

2. Write one fact, one opinion, and one inference for ¶5.

Fact: _____

Opinion: _____

Inference: _____

3. Write one fact, one opinion, and one inference for ¶10.

Fact: _____

Opinion: _____

Inference: _____

9 | Discussing the Issues

Answer the questions and discuss your answers with a partner.

1. Do you think savior siblings are a good idea? Why or why not?

2. According to Gregory Stock and John Campbell, genetic manipulations in humans will occur. Do you think there is anything that could or should be done to control such genetic manipulations?

3. If you could genetically enhance your child, yourself, or someone you loved, would you? If so, in what circumstances would you do it? If not, why not?

Putting It On Paper

A. Write a five-paragraph essay on one of these topics.

1. What are the three most important ethical concerns in medicine?

2. What are the three most important medical advances of the past 100 years?

Steps for your essay

    a. In your first paragraph, clearly state your opinion about your topic and your general reason or reasons why.

    b. Your second, third, and fourth paragraphs should each describe a separate ethical concern or advance that relates to your topic.

    c. In your final paragraph, summarize the ideas you state in your essay.

B. Exchange essays with a partner. First, read your partner's essay and answer the questions in the checklist. Then give feedback to your partner.

> **NOTE**
>
> Each of your paragraphs should contain a main idea that is supported by details—facts, data, examples, etc.—that prove or illustrate your main idea.
>
> For more on *supporting details*, see page 77.

✔ CHECKLIST

1. Does ¶1 show your partner's opinion about the topic?
2. Do the three body paragraphs each contain a separate concern or advance?
3. Does the final paragraph summarize the ideas contained in the essay?
4. Does each paragraph contain a main idea?
5. Do the details of each paragraph support the main idea?
6. Are you persuaded by your partner's recommendation or opinion?
7. Is there any information in the essay that is not related to your partner's topic? If yes, please underline it on your partner's essay, and write it below:

_____

_____

_____

_____

_____

C. Revise your work based on your partner's feedback.

Taking It Online | A Question of Ethics

A. With a partner, use the Internet to research ethical and unethical medical practices.

ONLINE TIP

Try your search on more than one search engine. Different search engines turn up different results.

1. Discuss with your partner what you consider ethical in medicine or medical research.

2. Use Google (www.google.com) or another major search engine to begin your online research.

3. Search for websites with information about two medical practices that you consider ethical and two that you consider unethical. You may find some of these terms useful:

ethical/unethical	medicine/medical
experiment/-ation	research
gene/genetic	responsible/irresponsible
laboratory animal	science/scientific
life-saving	test/testing

4. Preview the websites.

B. Complete the table with the information that you find.

Ethical Medical Practices	
Name:	Name:
Type of activity or practice:	Type of activity or practice:
Website:	Website:
Reason:	Reason:

Unethical Medical Practices	
Name:	Name:
Type of activity or practice:	Type of activity or practice:
Website:	Website:
Reason:	Reason:

C. Following up. Discuss your research with the class or in small groups. Think of three actions you could take to support the ethical medical practices or demonstrate your concern for the unethical medical practices you found.

Vocabulary Index

Skills and Strategies Index

Reading Skills

Vocabulary Strategies